Adam's Blunder

Adam's Blunder

The highest expression of humanity is not to please God, but to agree with Him

GRAEME SCHULTZ

Gobsmacked Publishing

All Scripture quotations, unless otherwise indicated, are taken from the Holy Bible, New International Version®, NIV®. Copyright ©1973, 1978, 1984, 2011 by Biblica, Inc.™ Used by permission of Zondervan.

All rights reserved worldwide. www.zondervan.com The "NIV" and "New International Version" are trademarks registered in the United States Patent and Trademark Office by Biblica, Inc.™

Copyright © 2018 by Graeme Schultz

First published March 2018

All rights reserved. No part of this publication may be reproduced, distributed or transmitted in any form or by any means, including photocopying, recording, or other electronic or mechanical methods, without the prior written permission of the publisher, except in the case of brief quotations embodied in critical reviews and certain other non-commercial uses permitted by copyright law. For permission requests, write to the publisher, addressed "Permissions Coordinator" at the address below.

Graeme Schultz/Gobsmacked Publishing

19 Trotters Lane
Cudgee, VIC 3265, Australia

Email: graeme@design2build.net.au

www.gobsmackedpublishing.com.au

Cataloguing-in-Publication Data

Author: Schultz, Graeme

Email: graeme@design2build.net.au

Title: Adam's Blunder

Subjects: Devotional

Adam's Blunder

Graeme Schultz

ISBN 9780994603081 (paperback)

ISBN 9780994603098 (ebook)

Typeset by bookbound.com.au

Dedication

There are several people who I wish to acknowledge
for their help in enabling me to complete this book.

My wife Angela

Your encouragement and belief in me is worth so much more
to me than you will ever know.

Our daughter Amber

You committed yourself to the marathon task of editing,
this book is so much better for your input.

Friends and Family

Angela and Harmony thank you for proof reading.

And for the many who have expressed your support along the way,
knowing that you value my writing keeps me at it.

Contents

Introduction		ix
Chapter 1	Questions	1
Chapter 2	The Way we Were	4
Chapter 3	Broken	8
Chapter 4	Crucified	12
Chapter 5	Adam's Legacy	14
Chapter 6	The Eyes of the Heart	19
Chapter 7	Knowledge	22
Chapter 8	Created in God's Image	24
Chapter 9	Adam's View of God	27
Chapter 10	The Original Adam	32
Chapter 11	Faith	38
Chapter 12	Dead in Christ	41
Chapter 13	The Divine Nature	45
Chapter 14	The Better Way	47
Chapter 15	Too Good to be True	53
Chapter 16	The Soul	57
Chapter 17	The Spirit	61
Chapter 18	To Agree with God	67
Chapter 19	Freedom	71

Chapter 20	Seeing and Knowing	75
Chapter 21	Uncertainty	80
Chapter 22	Walking in the Spirit	84
Chapter 23	The True Me	88
Chapter 24	A New Way to Live	91
Chapter 25	The Adventure	96
Chapter 26	My Genius	99
Chapter 27	The Light	102
Chapter 28	The Glory	106
Chapter 29	A New Identity	111
Chapter 30	Clean	116
Chapter 31	In the Light	119
Chapter 32	God's Plan	122
Chapter 33	Dominion	125
Chapter 34	My Restful Design	130
Chapter 35	Courage	134
Chapter 36	Eternity	138
Chapter 37	The Cross	143
Chapter 38	My Name	146
Chapter 39	Two Voices	149
Chapter 40	Unburdened	152
Conclusion		156

Introduction

My purpose in writing this book is to explore some of the fundamental opinions and paradigms which are widely accepted in Christianity, to shine the light on them, and consciously determine if they reflect the real truth as expressed in the life, death, and resurrection of Jesus.

My focus is not on any particular person or denomination, quite the contrary – my focus is simply on Jesus, who he is, what he did, and who we are as a result.

Please forgive my tendency to move between the first, second, and third person as I explore the subject. I hope it's not too distracting as I write from my personal experience, to the wider context, and back again.

You will also notice that as I progress into the book I employ a simplification in my use of gender and plural. I often refer to Adam and Eve as just the singular 'Adam', to simplify the flow as I articulate my thought process. Similarly I often employ the term 'man' as the collective of all humankind. My intention is not to be gender specific, but again, to simplify the narrative. This may not properly represent the thinking of everyone, but I ask for your indulgence as you read on.

Coming to terms with a new perspective is challenging stuff; it can be stretching, and possibly even make us mad enough to throw this book away, but also, hopefully give us a fresh perspective. If you experience these emotions then you are a part of the majority (the group that I am in), the group who highly value all that has contributed to their present point of view, yet quietly long for a deeper, more profound walk with God.

So I invite you to come with me in to Christ, not the Christ on the stain glass window or the one in the prayer from our childhood, but the one who lives in us so profoundly that we have been melded into one new being.

CHAPTER 1
Questions

Asking questions is not a bad thing.

It's probably one of the best ways to get to the truth.

I wasn't sure if I was allowed to ask questions, particularly ones that might take me beyond the pale – the status quo seemed so set in stone. I felt unsure of myself, and even a little bit wayward, the first time I started to explore thoughts about my Christian faith that were off the beaten track.

All of that's behind me now, I'm not fearful anymore – because I'm learning to trust that the Holy Spirit knows what He's doing. He is good at His job description of revealing the truth about Jesus. I'm realising from experience that He wanted me to pursue truth for myself all along; He doesn't seem to have as big a problem with it as I did.

Sometimes it's best to ask the hardest question first.

Sometimes it's best to take a leap over the incidental stuff and square-up to the biggest question you can think of… and test the popular truth to see if it's really worth having.

I'm not talking about questions that aren't going to affect things much, like; dress in church, worship styles, or leadership structures – I'm talking about questions that have the potential to completely undo the most foundational aspects of our faith. Questions that cause us to re-build again from the ground up.

Don't get me wrong; I'm not suggesting there is anything out of order with the essential message of our salvation in Christ. I am however, suggesting that there is a whole lot we have simply accepted on a foundational level, without actually passing it through our own personal truth filter.

So what would such a question look like? *What would qualify as the hardest question?*

In my view the hardest question of all for a Christian is this; "Does my faith really represent the way God meant it to be?"

Or to put it another way; "Has modern Christianity got it right? Is my personal belief system supposed to be this way – as delivered to me by the great big culture called 'Christianity'?"

I told you it was a big question!

'What's to be gained?' you may be thinking; 'And what happens if I do ask the hardest question … and discover a different answer to my previous point of view?'

THE ADVENTURE OF A LIFETIME IS ALL!

Asking the big questions can be like casting ourselves adrift, we don't know where we might end up, and we don't know whether it will have been worth the cost. Yet, if by chance we find ourselves in a new place of refreshing and joyful delight in God, then the cost will seem incidental and we will wonder why we didn't do it sooner.

Besides, not asking the biggest question could mean that we miss out on the best. It could mean that we settle for average. *Life's too short for average.*

I think I would rather be carried aloft on the wings of God, than live out my days in the safe harbour of normality. I don't want to be normal, I want to know God deeply and profoundly, I want my life in God to be as real as it can possibly be.

For that to be so – the hardest question must be asked.

In back of the notion that 'the hardest question must be answered', is the nagging thought that something is not quite right. That there has got to be more to Christianity than the neatly packaged lines, and the familiar well-used language.

It's a nagging thought that the clichés and catch-phrases of Christianity are not lining up with the reality of our lives. That, as much as we repeat the Christian jargon, we don't seem to be drawn any closer to the claims it makes.

At times it can seem as if the reality of our lives is more caught-up in the appearance of spirituality, than the actual fact of it.

In the cold light of day a question begins to form at the back of our minds. It's a big question, the biggest of them all, and for that reason we delay it – it's just too unsettling to confront.

It's the question I asked at the beginning; "Have we got this whole 'Christianity thing' right?" "Have we missed something that would bring all the jargon of Christianity into the realm of reality?" and, "Is such a thing even possible?"

If it is possible; if there is a Christianity out there that shifts all the language that is so familiar, from mere speculation to daily reality, then we would be mad not to ask the question.

From this point on, this book assumes that you are asking the question.

CHAPTER 2
The Way we Were

To ask such a question sets us on a journey into the foundations of how we modern day believers have packaged-up our belief system – *'why it is, what it is'*. It is an examination of what it is that holds us in a form of Christianity which is more comfortable with the appearance of spirituality, than the actual reality of it.

Big statement; stay with me now.

To conduct that examination, we must journey all the way back to our great, great, great… grand-daddy, Adam. With a clearer understanding of Adam's actions, we can better understand the legacy that he left us. In fact; unless we understand what actually took place back at the beginning, we will continue to unwittingly perpetuate its outcomes.

Let me explain that statement: Something broke inside humanity when Adam walked out of the Garden of God. It was humanity's 'in-built God compass' that was broken, and we can't find our way back to God without it. The only device available to us is the one that Adam constructed in its place; a flesh-made scheme that depends on the information generated by the natural realm as our means of locating the Truth about God.

Adam broke our spirits, and we have been seeking God by the means of the flesh ever since.

The problem is, our flesh is not up to the task, and no matter how sophisticated our efforts become, or how modern our religious practises, we too are stuck in Adam's folly unless we gain a fresh perspective of the way things were before Adam pulled the blinds down on the realm of the Spirit.

To understand this properly we need to examine that moment in human history when sin entered in. We need to get a handle on what actually took place when Adam and Eve sent the human race on a course separate from

God's presence. Only then we will be able to come to terms with our plight in the present day.

> **The case I want to make is that Adam and Eve were an entirely different kind of being prior to sin / than after sin.**

Their outward appearance may have been the same, but that is not what I am talking about, that is simply the earth suit that they wore in the natural realm. The 'real person' I am referring to is the spirit of a man, that part of us that lives in the spiritual realm and relates to God. The spirit person is not as easily perceived, as we are so used to looking to our five senses and our intellect to connect with reality. In other words, if we can't see it, or feel it, or understand it – then it doesn't exist. The spirit does not operate on that level; its information is spiritual information which is gained from an entirely different realm.

> **Our spirit exists in a realm beyond the perception of our senses.**

Remember the story in Luke 8:54-55 *(BSB)* when Jesus healed the little girl, "But Jesus took her by the hand and called out, 'Child, get up!' Her spirit returned, and at once she got up. And He directed that she be given something to eat". Her spirit, the real person, left her body when she died, and came back again when she was raised up.

From this we know that while our body is alive, our spirit is there, though it has no physical form. Yet, when our body dies our spirit continues to live-on apart from our body, in the realm of the spirit.

It is broadly accepted that we are a tri-partite being. Three parts in one being – spirit, soul and body.

Our spirit is the real person, it lives in the spiritual realm; it is our spirit that knows God.

Our soul is made up of our intellect, emotions, personality, natural abilities and characteristics.

Our body is simply our earth-suit; it carries us around in the realm of nature.

It's hard to shake-off the preconceptions that we have about our spirit and soul. In the past I thought of my soul as a kind of invisible oval-shaped lump inside me, somewhere near my belly, and my spirit as an ethereal shimmering ghost that followed me around. I am learning that my spirit and soul are much more than this, and this knowledge helps me to understand what Jesus has accomplished in me.

We don't talk much about our spirit, but it's necessary to understand exactly what our spirit is. Then we can understand how Christ rectified the calamitous actions of Adam. Our spirit has no physical attribute, it is completely non-physical, yet, it is our real self, *the true me*. It is who I am, in a much more real sense than my body. My spirit lives in a realm quite apart from nature. It transcends the natural realm – and it knows God.

At the beginning of the book of Revelation the Apostle John says 'I was in the Spirit on the Day of the Lord' – he had learned to lean back into Jesus, and fix his gaze upon the amazing reality which was returned to him at the cross. He didn't leave his body, it's not like that, he simply rested in the truth of Jesus, and identified himself in all that Jesus had accomplished. He chose to believe in a reality that was greater than the one on display in the realm of nature.

Our soul is much more familiar to us. We relate to it, and through it, as we live out our daily lives on planet earth. We are familiar with our soul because it operates through our senses and our intellect. We instinctively live our lives on the basis of our soul – our personality, emotions, likes and dislikes are all actively connecting us with life as our soul directs us. Our soul is very aware of our body, it directs our body, and gains its identity from our body image, natural abilities, and personal characteristics.

When God created Adam, He created him as a spirit that was 'alive' to Him. Adam's spirit knew God and fed on the life and love which proceeded from God. His spirit did this instinctively because it was designed that way – it was as natural as breathing is for the body. The environment in which Adam's spirit existed was God, God filled everything, and Adam simply lived off the heartbeat of God. His spirit was nourished and satisfied by the presence of God, and this kept Adam's spirit in a state of vitality and life.

When Adam & Eve decided to eat from the Tree of the Knowledge of Good and Evil they made a decision with spiritual ramifications. They decided to draw their nourishment from their own deeds, their own management of 'good and evil' – instead of the life and love that God provided.

They became independent beings – once in perfect union with God / now separated from God by their choice to be sustained by their own self-life. As a result their spiritual union with God died. God warned them that this would happen in Genesis 2:17 "But you must not eat from the Tree of the Knowledge of Good and Evil, for when you eat from it you will certainly die". He warned them that they would die *spiritually*.

There is no spiritual life, but for the life that proceeds from the heart of God. As soon as Adam and Eve chose to be nourished by their attempts to generate life through their own efforts and good deeds, their spirits died.

(For simplicity I will refer to Adam & Eve as the singular 'Adam' going forward – so when you read 'Adam' assume I am talking about both, unless otherwise noted.)

CHAPTER 3
Broken

Adam's spirit depended on the spiritual nourishment of God's presence to retain its vitality; without that nourishment it had no life-source.

Once Adam's spirit died, humanity was broken. We became a different being than we were at the beginning. We became a being with a dead spirit.

Where it had once received nourishment from the heart of God, this new being now had to depend on its soul for sustenance (its spirit had no life to offer), it had to look to *itself* for its identity and sense of worth.

Once the spirit was side-lined the soul became the real person – and so this new being was directed by its intellect and five senses, instead of the Spirit of God.

The soul became the real me.

The soul of Adam was his unique mix of characteristics given to him by God. It gave expression to the inner life of Adam. When his spirit was alive it expressed that divine life, but once his spirit had died it was left with no spiritual life as the basis for this expression, and so its expression was limited to the natural realm.

Without a living spirit to inform it, the soul of humanity is restricted to the information presented to it by its five senses, intellect and personality. This information is gathered from the soul's observations of the physical realm and the soul then forms a response. It considers the circumstances, and the values of the physical realm, and responds with its own unique management of the 'good and evil' equation.

It was akin to asking the brain to perform the tasks of the heart. The human brain is for thinking, not for pumping our life-blood. And the human soul is for expressing our unique personal characteristics, not for generating spiritual life.

God created Adam as a spirit-directed being,
and Adam re-made himself as a soul-directed being.
His identity and worth was given freely from the heart of God,
but Adam opted to construct a poor copy from his own deeds.

This was not an upgrade.

This new being was so inferior to the original that there was barely any resemblance at all, only its physical appearance remained unchanged.

Imagine a Formula-1 racing car; it is the most spectacular of all road machines. Now imagine removing the engine and all its management systems and installing a rubber band in their place, they may still look the same on the outside, but that is the end of the comparison – they are now two completely different machines.

Such is the comparison between the man created in God's image and the man re-engineered by Adam.

For much of my life I didn't understand this difference, I didn't know that Adam recreated the human race. I thought there was no difference between the pre-sin Adam and the human race that followed, but for the fact that he hadn't yet committed his first sin. It never occurred to me that the version of humanity that God created in His own image was so totally broken by the actions of Adam, that the resulting man was just a shell of his former self.

In reality, my understanding of that earlier version of man was viewed through my own 'fallen-nature glasses', I viewed Adam as a man who had always lived within the constraints of the flesh. I thought he was *created* soul-directed, not spirit-directed, **and that God had made us all that way.**

This impression of the initial design of humanity had skewed my understanding of the human dilemma; I had limited the problem to be all about our **deeds**, when in reality it is all about our **nature**.

If we are to go beyond a culturally-based Christianity, towards a living-faith-based Christianity, it's important to clearly differentiate between these two models of humankind.

Let's spend a few minutes contemplating this. God told Adam not to eat from the Tree of the Knowledge of Good and Evil, if he did he would surely die. In Genesis 3:4 the serpent claims he would not die, but that his eyes would be opened, and he would be like God, knowing good and evil. (Satan often presents his lies with a twist of truth in them so they are more believable.) Adam would indeed become like God, knowing good and evil, but implicit within that knowledge was the obligation to be holy just like God, and if he wasn't holy – then he would die.

This is the scam that satan conned Adam into believing; that just like God he had the ability to generate his own righteousness. That is what 'knowing good and evil' is all about; it imposes on us the imperative to measure up. Adam was created as a man who received righteousness from God for free. Just by being in union with God it was automatically transferred to him. Once he knew about good and evil, he set himself (and all of us that followed) the task of generating our own righteousness.

> **The imperative to measure-up was Adam's idea, not God's.**

Adam couldn't do it and neither can we. We don't have a built-in righteousness-generating nature – the soul is not made of such material. We were designed to receive righteousness from the heart of God as we hide ourselves in the love and life that flows freely from Him.

Adam set for humanity a role that we were not designed for, 'that we would carve-out a life of self-worth from our individual management of good and evil'. He removed the formula-1 engine (the Holy Spirit) from us, and destined us to produce a God-pleasing life from a rubber band propulsion system – sure this system might produce a few km/hr of good works, but that would hardly rate in comparison with true Godly righteousness.

The really tragic part is that humanity has been attempting to please God without the slightest chance of doing so ever since. And we didn't even know it.

> **So the difference between pre-sin Adam,**
> **and all of humanity that followed,**
> **is that Adam's righteousness was not measured by his right living,**
> **but by his union with God.**
> **A union which automatically transferred righteousness**
> **from God to Adam**
> **as Adam participated in God's divine nature.**

It was this basic characteristic of humanity that Adam broke.

Adam took the God part (the divine nature of man), and exchanged it for a flesh nature. He de-commissioned the spirit, and in its place inserted the soul – and humanity has been attempting to reach God through the means of the flesh ever since. Not the 'flesh' in terms of our physical flesh and blood, but the self-dependant 'flesh nature' which became the propulsion system of the soul-based man.

All that I have described here is the condition of humanity without the work of the cross. It is a description of the utter helplessness of humanity to resolve their plight, because it was about more than a just record of sins committed, it was about a race of beings who 'by nature' insisted that they be the solution to their own problem, *but couldn't.*

Adam re-made humanity without the ability to receive from God, because that flow only takes place within the context of union – it is only as we are 'one with God' that we can share in His life and love. Independence has no ability to share in this life-flow; we simply cannot please God through our own means. Yet, Adam built within us a mechanism that insists on the human contribution of self-made worth – it is our nature and legacy from Adam.

As we progress further through this book we will look more closely at human history and, in particular, the biblical account of man's attempt to please God through his lifestyle and religious observances – *the experiment of Adam played out on the stage of human history.*

But for now, I would suggest that the nagging thought I mentioned earlier 'something is not quite right', is a faint echo of the way it was before Adam derailed us.

Our spirits remember a better way.

CHAPTER 4
Crucified

Enter Christ.

What exactly did He accomplish on the cross?

Did He simply come as my scape-goat, and bear the punishment due to me? Or did He complete something far more than a sinner's hostage exchange? If it was all about standing-in for me and taking my penalty, then it is an external act – a ransom paid by Jesus so that I need not pay it. Like balancing the ledger of life, Jesus paid-off all my negative entries.

Or, did He come to crucify me with Him? Did He carry my 'dead-to-God' spirit onto the cross, and kill the 'old flesh me' who was incapable of reaching God? That's more than an act of benevolent payment. That is murder. Did Jesus murder the being that Adam created? That's not external anymore, that's as up-close and personal as it gets!

If this is so, it's a different Christianity than I thought, and my foundations really do need to be shaken so I can re-build on the truth. This is not just a small adjustment to my belief system, it's not just some minor tweaking to get the thing running more smoothly – this is a complete re-build, a totally new propulsion system.

Paul says in Galatians 2:20, "I have been crucified with Christ". Clearly not his physical self, but a more internal death. His spirit, which was God-less, was crucified, so that he could be re-born with a divine natured spirit.

This God-less spirit didn't go down willingly. It didn't meekly climb up onto the cross with Christ and submit to its self-destruction, it was incapable of participating in anything that would diminish its self-sustaining nature. The only possible solution was that it be profoundly, and mystically, crucified with Christ as He became the final Adam. In a very real sense,

Jesus became the whole of humankind. He suffered the punishment for the foolish experiment of Adam, and then He crucified the God-less spirit that this experiment produced. He included the entire human race in His crucifixion so that Adam's reign of terror could be finished once and for all.

*This spiritual slaughter was completed in every regard
on the cross 2000 years ago,
and we individually and personally receive it today
as we place faith in Jesus.
It is an eternal event which is translated to us
when we acknowledge our problem,
and step-in to Christ's solution.*

I use the term 'murder' quite deliberately, because it implies a violent act committed against an unwilling victim. Christ crucified our 'dead-to-God' spirits and we had no say in the matter – lest we claim some credit by way of willing participation, and perpetuate Adam's self-sufficient nature. We can only receive this as we realise that we having nothing to bring to the table, Christ has done it all and we simply lean-back into the new nature He has opened up for us.

Without this understanding we remain trapped in a life-long obligation to maintain our favour with God through our good living. With it, however, we are able to step back into the model of humanity that God first created. That's why Paul refers to us as a new creation in 2 Corinthians 5:17 *(BLB)*, "Therefore if anyone is in Christ, he is a new creation. The old things have passed away; behold, the new has come into being".

We have been recreated back to the original version, by the blood of Christ.

CHAPTER 5
Adam's Legacy

Now that we can see the difference between the pre-sin and post-sin man, we can look more closely at the issues facing humanity as a result of Adam's legacy.

Jesus has reconstructed humanity back to the original design, our spirits have been given the kiss of life, and we are in union with God again – *just like Adam was in the beginning.* You would think that we would embrace our new nature, and joyfully leave the old behind us like a deflated children's toy, but by-and-large we don't, because we can't see with clarity what the cross accomplished.

What is obstructing our view?

Our soul remains un-renewed!

Our soul remains locked in the thinking of Adam. Jesus rebirthed our spirit, but our soul must be retrained. Our soul is our property; it is our unique and personal make up. Nobody can make changes to it without our permission, **only we can choose to agree with God.**

Some people pray for God to give them human qualities like courage or patience, but these are ours to choose not His to give. He has already given us a renewed spirit, and it is up to us to choose to renew our minds in agreement with the condition of our spirit. Jesus crucified our God-less spirits without our permission, He just went ahead and did it, but our soul won't be renewed without our consent.

If we continue to think that God wants us to present Him with a life of good deeds and religious observance to *qualify* for His life and love, then we will never retrain our soul in the ways of the spirit. We are qualified by the blood of Christ alone, and our soul is renewed when it aligns itself with that spiritual reality.

Can you see the vicious cycle here? We need to receive the work of Christ to escape the legacy of Adam / but the legacy of Adam obstructs the work of Christ from our view. The ultimate outcome of this dilemma is that we attempt to view the work of Christ through the lens of Adam's un-renewed mind. This view of Christ is so distorted by Adam's way of thinking that we end up back where we started; trying to please God through our good living… *only now it has a Christian label on it.*

Jesus has done everything possible to return us to our original design; He has crucified every obstacle that would obstruct our return to the life of the Spirit – now it is up to us to bring our way of thinking into agreement with it.

The thinking we inherited from Adam is self-based. It is the same thinking that Adam employed when he set up the soul into the place of the spirit – *'my value is directly proportional to my conduct'.*

As long as we think in this way it is impossible for us to fully receive the free gift that Christ came to give. We cannot fully grasp the revelation of Christ with the same mindset that Adam developed to conceal it.

> **Our only hope is to take a leap into the unknown –**
> **we must do the most outrageous thing ever contemplated –**
> **we must begin to think like a dead person.**

I deliberately put it that way to shock you.

The mind of Adam bears no resemblance to the mind of Christ – yet it remains the preferred option in most sections of the Christian community the world over. This is because the alternative seems too far-fetched to even contemplate, *and also because Adam's legacy doesn't let go easily.*

How does a dead person think? A dead person has run out of options, he has come to the end of himself; he can do no more because time has run out – he has no choice but to surrender to the facts – he is now in God's hands.

> **The soul is finally renewed when we stop trying to please God**
> **and accept that His pleasure was never connected**
> **to our self-generated acts of goodness –**
> **it was always about whether we will rest in,**
> **and surrender ourselves, to His unconditional love.**

The pull of the soul is strong, and the thinking of Adam is compelling. We cannot conceive a different way to live – so the leap we must make defies every logical bone in our body. God wants us to stop trying to please him.

Stay with me now!

A disclaimer just in case you are thinking of throwing this book in the bin: God is pleased when we hide ourselves in the virtue of Christ. And when we do, good works well-up from His Spirit within us, His Spirit now living through us in a life of spontaneous godliness. God wants us to learn to walk in His free gift of righteousness, not to perpetuate the self-righteousness of Adam. It takes great courage to abandon our fears, lean-in to Him, and do it.

> **God is not opposed to our good works,**
> **but He is opposed to the security we draw from them –**
> **our right standing with the Father rests on Jesus shoulders alone.**

This makes no sense to the impulses of the soul. The soul always searches out the next option; it always looks for one more God-pleasing task. It never gives in, or gets to the end of itself – so the very thing that Christ came to do is delayed in the believer's life.

For years I was taught that God was observing my life in the hope of detecting behaviour that would please Him, *but nobody ever taught me how to really and deeply live by faith in Jesus.*

The challenge for the believer is to re-train the soul in the ways of the spirit (to deeply believe it), because the spirit knows Jesus very well. This knowledge is the game changer.

Remember my earlier description of the soul – it is our intellect, emotions, personality, natural abilities, and characteristics. Adam elevated the soul to a role it was never designed for, he decided to draw his security from the messages he received from these human attributes. He judged life according to the sense of well-being he experienced on an intellectual, emotional and personal level. He lifted his eyes off the love and life that God gave him for free, and fixed his gaze on the well-being he experienced in his flesh that resulted from his lifestyle choices.

His soul reported a continuous newsreel of how things were going. If his circumstances were pleasing, then he was happy, and his world was in order. If not, he lost his joy, and battled to make things right again.

If only he could silence his soul and hear the real truth – that he was the object of God's love, and as such, his circumstances were hidden in the goodness of God without him even earning it. He could have saved himself a great deal of stress and turmoil.

Our soul measures our value on the basis of our performance on this earthly stage; it is energized by our management of 'good and evil'. In the beginning, Adam didn't even know what 'good and evil' was; he had no concept of performance-based worth. His worth was based on something far superior to the vagaries of human behaviour – it was based on the nature of God living in him.

This performance-based thinking that we inherited from Adam is very established in us, we really can't imagine that life could operate any other way. It is the modus operandi of the whole world, every sphere of human activity and expression, is in some way tied up in it.

**Yet it is the thing that sets the people of God
apart from the rest of the herd –
we do not need to 'do good' to be good, rather,
goodness is transferred to us as we place faith in the goodness of God.**

This is the reason Christ came – not to perpetuate the self-made goodness of Adam, but to return us to the God-given goodness we were originally created with.

Can you see the difference?

I spent much of my life thinking that Jesus saved me so I could be good for God. I thought the whole thing was about pleasing God with a Christian lifestyle and religious commitment. I thought that God was disappointed with Adam when he sinned, and that Jesus came so that I could do better. My thinking was so broken that I continued on my merry way, attempting to please God on the basis of my virtuous life, just as Adam did. *Little did I realise, Jesus released me from that very thing so that I could live my life from a much higher truth.*

I received the message of salvation, and wove it back into the thinking of Adam, and produced a life that was no different to my old life, but for the external appearance of religion.

I reconstructed Christ to suit my own image, just like Adam had done to God all those years earlier.

Christ came to bring an abrupt end to the thinking of Adam; He came to arrest the compulsive obligations of the flesh as it attempts to generate its own self-worth – and to return us to the spontaneity and freedom of life in the Spirit that we were designed for. To do that, we must leave behind Adam's soul-based thinking, and rediscover the eyes of our heart, that Paul refers to in Ephesians 1:18.

CHAPTER 6

The Eyes of the Heart

"I pray that the 'eyes of your heart' may be enlightened in order that you may know the hope to which He has called you, the riches of His glorious inheritance in His holy people".

Christ came to re-open the spiritual eyes that Adam closed; He came to give us back the sight that Adam had at the beginning, before he embarked on the mad experiment of looking to himself for his identity and worth.

The outcome of having the eyes of our heart operating again is breathtaking. We begin to see the remarkable truth of who we are, our rich inheritance, and the glorious power which is ours in Christ.

You see, we do not lack anything –
we are simply unable to see what we have, and who we are.

The 'eyes of our heart' is something that most of us have no concept of. We are used to perceiving reality from the physical evidence, and we can't attach any physical evidence to the notion that our heart has eyes. Our heart is referring to the inner man or spirit, which is the real us.

This spirit-being can see, not with physical sight, but spiritual sight – *our true self can see God.*

Jesus spoke of this sight often in the book of John. John 5:19 *(NLT)* says, "I tell you the truth, the Son can do nothing by Himself. He does only what He *sees* the Father doing." Jesus could see His Father, and this sight enabled Him to do extraordinary things – He saw His Father with the eyes of His heart.

Adam also saw his Heavenly Father before he cut-off that sight. This sight was the spiritual sight which perfect beings spontaneously enjoy through the union they share with God. He had natural sight too, but that sight was not originally tuned-in to good and evil. In other words, his true identity and daily reality, was reported to him by his spiritual eyes – and his natural eyes simply took-in the wonder of the created environment he lived in.

In Genesis 3:7 we read, "Then the eyes of both of them were opened, and they realised they were naked". In their initial perfect condition their identity was not reported to them by their natural eyes, but by their spiritual eyes, and their nakedness gave them no cause for concern. Once they separated themselves from God, their natural eyes took over the job and reported a completely different reality; one based on their physical condition, not their spiritual one.

Adam and Eve were just as physically naked before they ate the fruit; the only thing that was different was their sight. Their original 'spiritual sight' did not record their physical condition as the measure of their worth, yet, their latter sight focussed-in on their physical condition... *the 'knowledge of good and evil' was born.*

Ever since Adam's exit from the garden, the great hoard of humanity has been looking to themselves for their sense of identity – even the religions that espouse inner enlightenment measure the behaviour of a man as the measure of his worth. It is all about our progress towards personal betterment. I cannot think of one religion or philosophy that is not based on the cycle of personal improvement which is necessary for adherence to their particular creed.

This perspective is completely out of place in the Christian context – we are good because Christ gives us goodness, *that is all*. Any resultant expression of goodness in our lives is simply the overflow of Christ within. We fix our eyes on Christ, and rivers of living water overflow from us as a result – not because we copy His example, but because He crucified the man that would attempt to self-generate godliness, and gave us His divine life in its place.

John 7:38 says, "Whoever *believes* in me, as Scripture has said, rivers of living water will flow from within them".

It is where the Christian faith differs from all the others, *(or at least should differ)* – only Christians have the eyes of their heart opened. But unfortunately, most continue to prefer the eyes of the soul, and so, in reality we often differ very little.

This statement is not intended as a wholesale criticism of Christians, but rather a wake-up call that we possess so much, yet only realize such a meagre amount of our true self. We have been reborn as spiritual giants, identical siblings to Jesus, and yet we settle for mere servitude and the appearance of religion.

All because the eyes of our soul are reporting an inferior reality to us.

The real problem here is that most Christians have no problem with allowing the soul to be in charge of their flow of information, *as though God meant it to be that way.* They are quite content to measure their personal well-being according to their performance and circumstances in the natural realm.

CHAPTER 7
Knowledge

Unless the soul has been through the renewal process described in Romans 12:2, it can only report on lifestyle and religious adherence. The human soul arrives at the point of salvation with a blank page in relation to spiritual things; it has no capacity to discern truth until it begins to see for itself the stunning vista which is constantly on view before the born-again spirit. It has not yet learnt to elevate spiritual truth (the truth which is experienced by our spirit), to superiority over natural truth (the truth our soul perceives in the natural realm).

*Christ re-birthed our spirit,
and we bring our soul into agreement.*

Our spirit was returned to the presence of God, it is acutely aware of the transformation in us as a result of the sacrifice of Jesus, and our soul joins in as it embraces the reality which is clear to our spirit.

Paul was speaking to born-again believers in his Romans 12:2 exhortation, "be transformed by the renewal of your mind". Their spirit was already transformed by the blood of Jesus, that was a done deal – but their soul was theirs to control, and could be only transformed by bringing it into agreement with the work already accomplished by Christ's blood.

What exactly did their spirit know that their soul didn't?

Their spirit knew that Jesus had completed His mission. He had destroyed the self-natured being which Adam constructed to manage good and evil, and in its place re-birthed humankind back into the original design – *our spirit can see this as plain as the nose on our face.* Our spirit is not attempting to construct a theological position to support this view, not at all – our spirit simply lives in this environment for every moment of every day, it is the atmosphere of its existence.

And it calls our soul to live there too by faith.

Our spirit doesn't tell our soul to try harder, or to do more religious things to achieve this lofty place – quite the contrary; our spirit simply tells our soul to rest in this truth. It is not something we do, but something we see – and having seen it, we simply cast ourselves headlong into it.

One thing holds our soul back from such a radical step: its ability to see spiritual truth has been so damaged by the legacy of Adam that it can barely glimpse the magnificent spectacle which is 'Christ in us'. Instead it settles for mere lifestyle-based religion.

This is the mystery that Paul speaks of in Ephesians and Colossians, 'Christ in you'. It's a mystery because the soul has lived without it since Adam stepped out of God's presence. But now that we are back where humankind started, we are in God's presence, and the mystery has been solved. We are hidden with Christ, in God – Colossians 3:3.

Our spirit knows it, and longs for our soul to catch-on. Our soul catches on as it grasps the magnitude of Christ's gift of life, and lets go of man-made religious activities to have it.

CHAPTER 8
Created in God's Image

Growing up, I was often told that I was the image of my dad. I think it was mostly to do with my physical appearance, but also possibly some personality traits. To be honest, I couldn't really relate to it, and even now, I don't see what other people saw. It could be that those who said it knew my dad as a boy and young man, and related to me from that perspective – but I didn't know him as a boy and only saw photos of him as an adult.

Being created in 'God's image' can be similarly elusive.

It's hard to connect any likeness between the holy and majestic being who is God, and the flesh and blood man we know as Adam (and ourselves).

We know from Genesis 1:26-27 that God decided to make man in His own image, in fact 'in His own likeness'. Yet God was not a physical being, so the likeness can't be referring to that. We can only conclude that this likeness was a spiritual thing – that we were made out of the same spiritual substance as God.

This being that God created in His own image, was like God, because he was a perfect spirit just like God. Adam was a spirit, *who also lived a physical life.* And God also related to the physical realm, God was a Spirit, and the realm of nature was a continual display of His supernatural wonder and majesty.

It was all so wonderfully natural for Adam; God was in, and through everything – and Adam related to God spontaneously and freely as a spirit-man. A man who lived in the realm of nature, and the realm of the spirit, seamlessly.

If we are to grasp the thing that Christ accomplished on the cross, then we must understand this existence that Adam first enjoyed. Adam did not need to come into God's presence or deliberately engage with God – God was the atmosphere and totality of his entire existence. Adam's spirit breathed-in the life of God just like we breathe air. There was no separation, no need to choose to spend quality time with God – God was his home, he lived in God and he knew it, and revelled in it.

Don't confuse Adam's 'walk with God in the cool of the day' as an appointment Adam kept with God to spend quality time together – that was a post-sin phenomenon. Adam could only perceive the natural realm after the fall *(the spiritual realm was lost to him),* and so God met him there.

And so it was that Adam did indeed sin, he walked away from his union with God and set-up house with his soul in charge. At that moment in time his spirit died, just as God had said it would in Genesis 2:17. We can also see this fact clearly expressed in the New Testament; Romans 5:12 *(NAS)* says, "Therefore, just as through one man sin entered into the world, and death through sin, and so death spread to all men, because all sinned."

This was not the physical death which ultimately befalls all humankind, but the death of our spirit as expressed in Ephesians 2:1 *(GNT),* "In the past you were spiritually dead". Our spirit died because Adam cut us off from the nourishment that comes from living in the atmosphere of God's life and love, just as our physical body also dies when it is cut off from the nourishment of food, water and air.

In a very real sense Adam starved the collective spirit of humankind to death when he chose to be nourished by his own good v. evil life, as opposed to the life he had for free just by being in God. He cut humanity off from the spiritual life-flow which was the very essence of 'being in the image of God' and the original man was broken. And so Adam constructed a new soul-based man in its place.

Imagine for a moment this man who was created in the image of God – he had a spirit that breathed-in the spiritual vitality of the atmosphere of God, and a body that breathed-in the life-giving clean air of the natural realm. These maintained his spirit and his body in perfect health, they provided for his life-source, and the result was a perfectly balance spirit-man.

Now imagine that this spirit-man decided to draw his spiritual life-source from an alternative place. He would now live off his own ability to generate virtue. He would breathe the spiritual atmosphere of his own self-made goodness, and be nourished by his own image, and as a result his spirit died of starvation.

The man 'in the image of God' was dead;
the image of the flesh was substituted in its place.

Adam sent humanity wandering in the wilderness of human effort for millennia. He set us a task we had no hope of completing – manufacturing our own righteousness from the emptiness of the soul. We were designed to breathe-in righteousness from the heart of God, not self-generate it from our own lifestyle, good deeds and religious practices.

CHAPTER 9

Adam's View of God

It's easy to fall into the trap of thinking that Adam's problem was that he committed the sin of disobedience – *God gave him just one rule and he broke it*. However, when we think that way, we cast both Adam and God in the wrong light.

God's instruction 'not to eat from the Tree of the Knowledge of Good and Evil' was not a command like the Ten Commandments, but a warning – much the same as warning a child not to cross a busy street… *serious consequences were at stake*. To suggest that God set Adam a command that He knew (in His Godly omniscience) that Adam would fail to satisfy, is to set God up as a cruel ogre, that He toys with humanity like a divine plaything. We can't have it both ways, God is either 'love' as He claims in 1 John 4:8, or He is nasty and malicious. We must be careful not to assign to God the characteristics of satan.

This is where the broken perceptions of Adam are at their worst, we read about the curse that was upon Adam as a result of his sin, and assume that God cursed him. Once again we assign to God a characteristic which is not true to Him – the curse was the natural overflow of Adam's decision, God was simply describing to Adam, what Adam had chosen for humanity. It was the curse of self-generated righteousness – *and it was way beyond us to generate our own righteousness*.

The truth is, even before Adam had sinned, God had crafted his salvation. In Revelation 13:8 we read that Jesus is the 'Lamb that was slain before the foundation of the world'.

> *In the heart and mind of God,*
> *Jesus had already gone to the cross for our sins*
> *before we even committed them –*
> *it was an eternal fact that was simply waiting*
> *for the realm of time to catch up.*

So God did not set Adam up to fail. He did not give him one rule to test his obedience. He knew Adam's choice to be independent long before Adam did himself, and He constructed a love-made salvation for us in advance. This is the heart of God. We must digest this character of God and lose ourselves in its fidelity, lest we fear God as a harsh, unyielding overlord, and never discover His true nature.

The broken (old) nature of humanity perceives God through the lens of its brokenness. Or to put it another way – the man that was first created in God's image, re-created himself, and consequently re-created everything in his world – *including God*. Of course we cannot re-create God, but we can adjust our view of Him to agree with our broken thinking.

The ultimate outcome of this broken thinking is that we have packaged God into a being that best suits our human insecurities; we have re-made Him in our own image.

This way of perceiving God is the beginning of idolatry – we worship such a distortion of God's true character that it is not the true God at all. It is a god we have set-up in our own image. We have taken the truth of God and filtered it through our self-made identity. And the god we worship as a result barely represents the true God at all.

This is a shocking claim to make – it won't win me universal popularity.

But popularity is not my objective, in fact; popularity may just be a part of the problem – the human need to be accepted by our peers can blind us of the truth. And if truth is the cost, then acceptance is not worth having.

Jesus didn't seek popular approval – in John chapter 6 many of His followers deserted Him, declaring 'this is a hard teaching, who can accept it?' It seems to me that if the gospel doesn't challenge our sense of reason to the very core, then it probably isn't the gospel. The gospel of Jesus Christ is shocking, it is scandalous to the thinking of Adam – 'Jesus saved us from ourselves, and we had no say in the matter'.

God did not give Adam an obedience ultimatum. He didn't give Adam one rule to see if he could hold the line. Quite the contrary, God articulated for Adam the consequences of 'going it alone', He made it very clear what was involved. And even though He knew Adam would not be able to resist the temptation to be god for himself, God crafted a salvation for us in advance that would ultimately return humanity to our original design.

God's warning to Adam was a love warning – 'don't choose independence, you will lose immeasurably more than you will gain. Living outside of my presence is an existence you don't want – don't go there!' God had no agenda for Adam but that he would live within the security of His love.

It's important that we shift our perspective of Adam's sin from 'disobedience' to 'independence'. If all Adam did was to disobey God then he remains exactly the same person before and after the fact, (but for having a criminal record). But if he chose independence from God then he cut off his true identity and nature, and crafted a new one that satan invented for him.

These are very different scenarios.

The condition of satan as expressed so clearly in Ezekiel 28:17, "Your heart became proud on account of your beauty, and you corrupted your wisdom on account of your splendour", is the same as the condition of Adam after he stepped out of God – he became proud of his identity in the flesh, and he corrupted the wisdom of his soul by elevating it to a place of splendour above the wisdom of God.

Even Adam's understanding of God's view of things was corrupted, Adam thought God was mad at him for sinning, but that barely rated compared to the real truth – God was staggered that Adam could walk away from His freely given love.

From day-one, Adam turned the camera back onto himself. As far as God was concerned it was never about Adam's choice to carve his identity out of his management of good and evil / but his choice to separate himself from the life and love that flowed from God's heart.

> **Adam put a price on God's love,**
> **and it almost broke God's heart,**
> **that His freely given goodness and mercy could be reduced**
> **to a commodity to be purchased with human effort.**

Adam's decision did not change God. We read in 2 Timothy 2:13, "If we are faithless, He remains faithful, for He cannot deny Himself". Adam's choice to be unfaithful to God did not cause an equal response from God in return, but it did cause Adam to lose sight of the true nature of God.

No matter what Adam did, God could not contradict Himself. He remained true to His love relationship with Adam – even if Adam had given up his spiritual sight, and could no longer see it.

God will be God – and we must determine exactly who He is.

If we switch off our spiritual sight and view God through the eyes of the soul, then He will appear to take on the persona that the soul has constructed for Him – *demanding judge, distant Lord, harsh ruler.*

If we switch off the eyes of the soul and view God through the eyes of our spirit, then we will see Him as He truly is – *lover, Father, nurturer.*

God does not have a split personality; He doesn't mess with our heads by changing His approach to us as the whim might take Him – never! **He is always loving, good and merciful.**

This has been the greatest thing that satan has accomplished on the earth; he has duped humanity into thinking that God responds to us according to the lifestyle we present to Him. It is so indelibly written into our DNA that we cannot conceive the alternative – that God responds to us because He is love, and if He didn't love us spontaneously and freely, then He would be denying His true self.

Satan knew he could not change God's love for us, so he did the next best thing and changed us (the objects of God's love). He is the master of all liars, and he conned us into thinking that God is conditional in His love relationship, and that it is conditional on our behaviour for that love to be expressed to us. It was satan's master-stroke, and the only way he could try to hurt God – he would attempt to obstruct the flow of God's love.

But God will not be manipulated by satan, by Adam, or by us – He will be true to Himself forever. His love is enduring and everlasting, it cannot be quenched. God's heart for us was even bigger than satan estimated, and He sent Jesus as an expression of His eternal love for humanity even before satan has released his first attack upon the integrity of God's love. Jesus became the 'lamb that was slain before the world began' because of God's unrelenting love, not merely as legal satisfaction of mankind's sin problem.

Jesus came because God is love – not judge.

Adam, and his offspring that followed, have attempted to cast God as the judge of humanity. We have placed a not-negotiable before God, 'judge me by what I do, not by who I am because of your great love' – and the history of the Children of Israel, and humanity at large, is the result.

God did not set Himself up as the judge of humankind, it's not the way He planned it. In fact, God didn't even intend for humanity to have a consciousness of good and evil. Satan attempted to get God to stop being God – *it was his best shot* – but all God did was turn-up the love even more, and He demonstrated this in the most astounding way possible – he chose to give up the life of His precious Son rather than tolerate satan's demands.

Twice in the book of John, in 3:17 & 12:47, Jesus declares that He did not come to judge the world, but to save it. Why would the Father judge the world if Jesus didn't? He and the Father are one – the only thing they judge is whether we are in union with His freely-given love and virtue, or independently attempting to generate our own righteousness.

> **It is essential then that God's people get comfortable with God's true character.**

It is equally essential that we gain a clear view of the work that Christ accomplished on the cross. Anything less than full and free access to the heart of God – His love, favour and blessing – is only partial Christianity. Jesus didn't go through the most horrendous suffering and death so that we would partially participate in its outcomes. He has given us Himself, His kingdom, and His great love – dare we take Him at face value and cast ourselves into Him with total abandon?

CHAPTER 10
The Original Adam

We are most likely to cast Adam in his post-sin nature rather than his pre-sin nature, as we attempt to understand his original design. This is because the nature that Adam gave humanity as their inheritance has effectively blocked out his original design from our view. However, we are able to build up a picture of Adam as a pre-sin man by looking at what the scriptures describe as our inheritance in Christ. The assumption being that Christ rectified the wrongs of Adam, and returned us to our original condition.

To do this we need to determine the purpose of Christ's coming and the resultant work that was accomplished.

If all Christ did in His coming was pay the penalty due to us, then Adam's condition and nature before there was sin, is of little consequence. It is of little consequence because the descendants of Adam that have walked the earth since that time can expect nothing more than a pardon for their mistakes. They cannot expect a wholesale change to their nature if Adam was effectively the same man before and after he sinned. There would be nothing to model a changed nature upon.

If Christ did more than pay the penalty for our sins and actually crucified our old-nature on the cross, then the condition of Adam before there was sin is of great importance – *because the pre-sin nature that Adam first enjoyed, is who we are now as we place faith in Christ's work.*

God is not in the business of experimenting with humanity the way Adam did. God made us perfectly the first time, and He re-made us perfectly the second time when Christ did away with our old nature. The only difference between the pre-sin Adam, and us as we live in union with Christ, is that Adam lived in an untainted world, whereas we live in a world damaged by sin. In every other regard we have been returned to the perfection of Adam.

There is only one kind of perfection, there are no degrees or variations – perfection means perfection. Adam was clearly perfect when God created him in His own image – and we also are perfect. Hebrews 10:14 *(ESB)* says, "by a single offering He has made perfect for all time those who are sanctified".

Just as there is only one kind of perfection, there is also only one kind of righteousness. Adam was clearly righteous at first; he didn't even know what good and evil were. We also were made righteous as 2 Corinthians 5:21 declares, "God made Him who had no sin to be sin for us, so that in Him we might become the righteousness of God".

In just the same way Adam also had 'life' in Him, a life that came from the breath of God. We also possess this same life, as Jesus declares in John 10:10 *(ESB),* "I came that they may have life and have it abundantly". Perhaps you've never contemplated that Jesus came to give you the same life that God gave Adam when He first formed him – *but don't discount it, it could be the most exciting news you will ever hear.*

Further to this, we know from Genesis 1:26 that God made Adam in His likeness, we also are re-made into Christ's likeness when we see Him as He is. As stated in 1 John 3:2, "But we know that when Christ appears we will be 'like' Him, for we shall see Him as He is". We are eternal beings already. We have crossed over from death to life (John 5:24). We are with Christ now and we have been made like Him.

Our spirit (the real us) has been re-made like the original.

I say all of this to break down the notion that Adam was effectively the same person before and after he sinned. If this thinking persists then we cannot grasp the new nature. We will always be restricted by the thought that Adam was created as a performance-based being, just like humanity is now *(but for the regenerative work of the cross).*

We will get to 'us' soon enough, but for now it is important to understand that the version of humanity that we see all around us is not the same as the model God created. Let's keep looking at this amazing creation of man.

Adam did not 'do' worship as we might do it now, he didn't have a 'time of intimacy with God', or shift his attention across to God from his other daily activities – Adam was 'in-God' and his spirit was constantly God-conscious. His spirit worshipped without ceasing as it always beheld

His throne. In Matthew 18:10 Jesus says that the children have angels who are always beholding the Father's face. This was also Adam's status, his spirit always beheld his Father's face, and worship overflowed.

> *We know that 'our spirit is the real me',*
> *the real Adam spent every moment*
> *in the glorious presence of his Father/God.*
> *It was the overwhelming fact of his existence.*

We also know that we have a soul which was corrupted by Adam's independence from God; this soul has taken the most beautiful love-union that existed between us and the Father, and sprinkled works of the flesh over it. Now we 'do' worship, instead of living in it. Now we come into God's presence by the means of a beautiful song or a gifted leader, instead of resting in the continual presence of the one who lives in us. Now we ask God to manifest himself, instead of allowing the indwelling reality of 'Christ in me' to be the manifestation.

Worship in the context of a church meeting is a wonderful thing, but God does not 'meet' with us because we have shifted our focus onto Him. He meets with us continually because the blood of Jesus has re-connected us – the same way He met with Adam in the beginning.

Adam's soul was a wonderful gift from God; it was the unique finger-print that God gave to Adam just so he could be a unique being – one of a kind. Had Adam remained in his union with God, then his soul would have revelled in God's presence just as his spirit did. His unique blend of personality, emotions and intellect would have marvelled at the wonder of God. In perfect unison his spirit and soul would have spontaneously expressed the joy of knowing, and being known, by God.

> *Without a living spirit to report the presence of God to Adam's soul,*
> *he had to find new ways to enter God's presence,*
> *and his soul obliged with man-generated religion.*

> *His soul constructed new ways to get God to show-up,*
> *his spirit had originally known a much better way;*
> *it had known how to rest in God.*

Let's not mistake this rest that Adam enjoyed before there was sin for idleness. Adam was not lazing in the deck-chairs of heaven; it's not that sort of thing. There was vitality and energy about Adam, but it didn't come from himself – it came from God's pleasure within him. This vitality overflowed into his soul, and his soul lived the most wonderful existence. This is the existence we read about in Paul's letters – 'he walked in the Spirit'. Adam's pre-sin soul was energized by his spirit's knowledge of God. It was the most productive, effortless way to live, because it was all generated by the heartbeat of God.

Imagine getting up in the morning and not contemplating a day full of obligations, juggling good and evil, and attempting to do the right thing by everyone – this was Adam's life. He was so absorbed in the magnificence of his union with God, that he just lived a great, big, loving and fruitful life.

God had no agenda for Adam, no particular plans and purposes – none of that was required, because as long as Adam had his eyes fixed on God, works of life from his Father's heart flowed through him. Jesus expressed this so beautifully in John 5:19, "The Son can do nothing by Himself; he can only do what He sees His Father doing" – that's the way it worked for Jesus (the last Adam) and that's the way it worked for the first Adam too.

Did Jesus have a window into heaven so He could watch what His Father was up to? Kind of; He had a living Spirit which was in perfect union with His Father. Not that the Father bossed Jesus around and told Him every step to take, but that He was so full of His Father's love that He lived out His Father's life on the earth.

Adam was just the same in the beginning. He didn't have to try to 'do' good because there was only goodness in him. As long as he had his eyes fixed on his Father, it just kept flowing out of him. It took a deliberate choice to look to himself for goodness, for that flow of life to cease. Adam's choice to self-generate goodness was a very big mistake – because he had no inherent goodness in him.

I love the way the Apostle Paul used word imagery to describe a spiritual truth, such statements as 'seated in heavenly places', 'joint heirs with Christ', 'hidden with Christ in God'. They all conjure up a picture of our true spiritual identity. But imagine the reality that Adam experienced – all of these word-images were his daily experience. He sat in heaven, he was con-joined to Christ, and was hidden in the Father with his divine brother Jesus – and how sad that he gave up such bliss all for the sake of 'being his own man'.

Yet, such is the potential that God built into us all, we are glorious beyond description as beings made in His image, to such an extent that we too can easily turn the spotlight off the creator and on to the created. We are truly magnificent, God's 'opus', His best work – and for that reason we must maintain our view squarely on God and not be distracted by our own amazing potential. Satan fell for it in Ezekiel 28:17, "You became proud on account of your beauty" – and ever since, he has been pulling the gaze of humanity away from God, and onto ourselves.

Does that mean God made a mistake in creating us as such magnificent beings? Would He have been better to make us a little less remarkable so we wouldn't get distracted by our potential? I don't think He could have done it any other way. He is perfect and He can't 'dumb-down' His work and still be pleased with the result. Better to let humanity pursue the mad experiment of Adam and ultimately redeem them back to their true selves. Better to have His beloved children choose Him as Father because they have finally grasped the scale of His love, than to have them hold-on to Him for lack of other options.

There was no risk here; God knew the outcome before He even started out. He never contemplated changing His design and creating human puppets, because in the end, He knew that His love, expressed so extravagantly at the cross, would pull us back in.

In His eternal mind it would be worth the wait.

In the last few pages I have been describing an environment, an eternal context in which God, Adam and the hosts of heaven exist. It is an environment that is so unlike the natural environment that we relate to on a daily basis, that we easily relegate it to the category of hopeful fantasy. Or at least, so far removed from us that it bears no serious consideration – it just doesn't seem relevant to the here and now.

If we are to grasp the inheritance that Christ gifted to us, then it is important that we come to terms with this environment. It is our true home now that Christ has breathed life back into our spirits. And even though we can't see it with our natural eyes, we must adjust our thinking so that it becomes our greatest reality.

It seems like such a leap to make that adjustment. It would mean denying the physical evidence in favour of the unseen – something we simply aren't used to doing.

In effect, we are attempting to undo thousands of years of Adamic thinking, and begin to operate in opposition to the daily newsreel that our natural eyes play over and over again before us.

Think of it this way; the natural realm is the small picture and the spiritual realm is the big picture. The small picture is contained within the big picture. The natural realm is real, but it is only a small part of the greater reality of our lives. We live in both realms, and the spiritual realm has the greater reality. We are used to assigning reality to things we can touch and see, the spiritual realm cannot be seen or touched in that way, yet the substance of it is greater than visible things.

As I said; this is a leap.

CHAPTER 11
Faith

I am suggesting that we begin to live in an environment we cannot see – the bible calls it faith.

You might be thinking; 'it just would not be possible for me to live that way' – and in response, I would say; 'you were designed to live that way'. It is in us, we are just so out of practice that it seems impossible.

Faith is not a demonstrative thing that we muster-up from within, and apply to a stubborn object; it is not dependent on our self-generated spiritual guts and determination. It is actually something we see with our spiritual eyes, and chose to make our greatest reality.

It's interesting that Jesus never castigated anyone for lack of prayer, only for lack of faith. Can you hear Him say to the disciples; 'where is your faith?' They couldn't exercise faith because they did not yet have the reality of the spiritual realm in focus. We modern Christians have turned faith into something we muster-up from within, and if we find that too hard we settle for prayer. Both faith and prayer are easy and restful if we can see the greater reality of the spiritual realm. All we are doing is conveying something that already exists from the big picture, into the small picture.

Most of the Christians I know (myself included) have lived our lives on the basis of the natural (or sense) realm, as our greatest reality. Unfortunately, this approach renders the spiritual realm as effectively irrelevant. Not that we have no regard for the spiritual realm, but rather we attempt to connect with the spiritual realm by the means of the flesh. We attempt to activate the realities of the spiritual realm by engaging in various habits, principles, processes and formula's – *these are the means of the flesh, not the spirit.*

For instance, we have been taught that God responds to our determination in prayer, our fervent worship, or our consistent bible study and quiet time habits. In reality, God responds to just one thing, our faith in the blood of

Jesus. Faith comes as we see the reality of the spiritual realm. We grasp the magnificence of Christ's work on the cross, and our resultant condition – and place ourselves unreservedly into that reality. And then our activities and works come as the overflow of that faith.

I cease from all the activities I once engaged in *to get* God's attention, and I rest in the crazy notion that He is already fully engaged with me through the indwelling Christ – only then can these activities become the joyful overflow of a vessel already full.

I choose to make the indwelling Christ the true me!

You might remember back at the start of this book I asked a question, "Have we got this whole 'Christian thing' right?"

We have arrived at the point where the rubber hits the road. By now you will realise, I am suggesting that we have been attempting to live in the spiritual inheritance which is already ours in Christ – *through the very means which required His sacrifice in the first place.*

We are attempting to access the realm of the spirit,
by the means of the flesh.

We are so distracted by all the things we need to do in this great big thing called Christianity, that we have lost the knack for being 'in-Him' and letting God do the doing.

This is serious.

My intention is not to be alarmist or to offend anyone; however, the salvation that Christ purchased for us is so astounding in its scope, that we must grasp hold of it fully. The blood of Christ has accomplished so much, and these accomplishments are ours, they are the very stuff of our existence. It defies logic for us to treat them as mere theological information, and hopeful speculation. They are the fact of who we truly are, and they call us to let go of the props that Adam set up around us *(those things that we do to gain access to God's favour),* and grab our true identity with both hands… by believing in the same truth that God sees in us.

At first, when this revelation began to change me, I felt a loss for all the wasted years. I was 55 years old as this started to happen – I would rather have had it all my life. But, at least I didn't get it in my nineties. Now I'm just glad that at last I can abandon my insecurities and let God do what He does best – love me. It's never too late to plunge into the new identity we have in Christ.

The idea that there is something inherently wrong with the way we have packaged-up Christianity is confronting to say the least, we have so much of our identity invested that it's hard to imagine embarking on an alternative course.

For that reason I want to lift the pressure off. This is not intended to destabilize you, but to give you a new hope and joy in the Lord that previously seemed unreachable. It is not intended to cause you to strive harder, or dig deeper, in a greater and more zealous response to the gospel. On the contrary, this is about learning to rest in a love that knows us better than we know ourselves, and loves us unconditionally regardless. It is about learning how to lean back into our new identity – 'Jesus in me'.

CHAPTER 12
Dead in Christ

In Galatians 2:20 *(ESV)* Paul says; "I have been crucified with Christ, it is no longer I who live but Christ who lives in me". It's easy to fall into the trap of thinking that Paul made that statement because of his unique calling and ministry – that Paul had crucified his flesh, and dedicated himself wholly to God's service. But when we read this scripture alongside the many others that refer to the 'death' experience of the believer it is clear that this is a universal truth, not limited to Paul alone.

Paul was actually explaining to us how the realm of the spirit works. He is saying that Christ took all of us up onto the cross with Him and we all experienced a mystical crucifixion. Jesus crucified the independent, old nature that separated us from God, so we could be re-born 'of God' – *just like Adam was in the very beginning.*

John 1:12-13 explains this beautifully; "Yet to all who receive Him, to those who believe in His name, He gave the right to become children of God – children born not of natural descent, nor of human decision or a husband's will, but born of God". By believing in Jesus our old soul-based lineage has ended, and we have been re-born of God. Not merely *by* God, or *for* God – but 'of' God. We have been re-born of Him, and re-made in His image, just like Adam – men and women in the likeness of God.

Some would say this is a positional truth, that it is true in principle. And now it's up to us to live up to it, to make it true in real-time on the earth. That is the kind of thinking that comes from the soul-man. The soul-man looks for the physical evidence to give credence to a spiritual truth. It puts the eyes of the soul above the eyes of the spirit and declares, 'This can't be true, just take a look at my less than perfect life! It may be true one day when I am in heaven, but it's far from true right now'.

The spirit-man sees a completely different perspective. He sees the blood of Christ crucifying all of the self-made securities we have constructed, and he sees Christ presenting us to the Father as perfect and holy children.

> **The difference between the soul-man and the spirit-man
> is where they go for their evidence.**

The soul-man looks at the natural realm and observes our meagre attempts at holiness – it deduces that we are far from the perfection of Christ. The spirit-man looks at the spiritual realm and observes the stunning accomplishments of the blood of Christ – it deduces that our frail human condition was no match for His sacrifice, and we have been made perfect without even lifting a finger to earn it.

This illustrates the point I made earlier about 'living in an environment we cannot see'. It is all about choosing to believe in the accomplishments of the blood of Jesus above the claims of the circumstances in our natural lives. And more than that even; it is about staking our very lives on this spiritual reality, such that we no longer entertain thoughts of unrighteousness and unworthiness.

> **We declare to ourselves loud and clear
> 'Christ's blood did enough, and I am the proof'.**

Does such a declaration make you squirm? Does it smack of ego and self-promotion? In reality the opposite is true – Christ's blood achieved the impossible, it turned the worst of sinners into the perfection of God, and all I did was let him.

Don't get me wrong, I still mess up, but it is a mess-up in the earthly realm only – I will never again be less than the perfection of Christ in the Father's eyes.

The thing I must never, ever, get wrong is to favour or elevate the works of Adam over the works of Christ. Adam may have defined humanity for some thousands of years, but Christ has defined humanity for eternity. My Adamic soul wants to hold on to me, it wants to contain me in the grasp of self-generated goodness. It wants me to be consumed with doing my best to please God. But my spirit knows better, it runs from Adam's legacy back into the atmosphere of God where it began. Like King David of old, it longs and faints for the courts of the Lord.

Jesus redeemed me completely from the foolish experiment of Adam, not partially or even mostly – He killed my Adamic nature as surely as Christ Himself was killed. And then I rose up anew in Him, never to be an individual again who strives to please God, now forever hidden in the one in whom God's pleasure rests forever.

Jesus is the new me, I do not exist other than in perfect union with Him, and His Father will never see me again other than through the work of the cross.

In the eternal mind of God, my individuality is lost in Christ.

God is not waiting for me to crucify my flesh and climb in; He crucified my flesh for me. He took my complacent, self-absorbed Adamic nature and commanded it to take its place in His sacrifice. This was no gentle Jesus – meek and mild, this was the Lord of Heaven declaring to my broken self that its day had come. Today is the day my Adamic nature would die its eternal death and never be raised up again.

I must not, and I will not, re-empower my old corrupted nature. Jesus killed it, and that settles it for me. From now on I go forward as a brand new creation, full of the divine life of God.

My view of this invisible realm may still be a little dim. The banquet of God's favour and love which is laid out before me is not yet completely clear to me, but this one thing I do know – as certainly as Christ died and rose up again, so also did I – into the newness of life.

In some respects it's easier to slip back into man-generated acts of righteousness. In some ways it's easier to determine to do good, rather than believe that Christ has made us good. It's a line in the sand. If we step over it, we can never be the same again because there are no half measures. Belief is an all-in thing, and we either fully believe that Christ did enough, or we believe in our own righteousness.

It's courageous stuff, casting caution to the wind and declaring ourselves holy. Don't do it if you are uncertain of Christ's sacrifice (that would be mere religion). But if you have stared at His cross, if you have contemplated that it was enough to destroy every remnant of your old self, then go ahead, leap in! Leap in to the life you were made for all those years ago in the garden – and re-made again years later by the blood of Jesus.

God has always seen us in Christ. Even in the lost millennia between the garden and the cross, His eternal mind has always known we were His treasured possession. Ephesians 2:5 *(BSB)* says, "But because of His great love for us, God, who is rich in mercy, made us alive with Christ, even when we were dead in our trespasses".

> *God didn't wait for us to ask,*
> *He didn't need us to reach out to Him,*
> *even in our deadness He had us in His heart*
> *and had our redemption in place.*

God didn't need our co-operation when we needed saving, and He doesn't need our 'personal best' to be spiritually alive now. He gives us life. Dare we grasp it? And live as the eternal beings we already are, though we remain for a just little while longer here on earth.

CHAPTER 13

The Divine Nature

The divine relationship we have with Christ is not something we readily grasp. We read scriptures such as 2 Peter 1:4 "…we participate in the divine nature", and skip over them without much fanfare. However, in so doing we miss the extravagance of our salvation – we have a new divine nature just like Jesus.

The reason we skip over this scripture, is that this scripture addresses the very thing that Adam broke. Adam re-made himself without a capacity to grasp the things of the spirit, and unless we over-ride that innate characteristic in us, we too will continue along those lines – and relegate spiritual truths to the category of irrelevant back-ground noise.

To a large extent that is the way modern Christianity approaches spiritual truths. We look for a context where they make sense in the natural realm, and if we can't find one we file them away as useful anecdotes, or handy lines to use when a Christian cliché is called for.

Sound harsh? I'm being as hard on myself as anyone else – I absorbed all the spiritual language and filed it away too, and then pulled it out of my bag of tricks when it was called for.

To 'actually' participate in the divine nature, is a whole new ball game; it's no longer about having a storehouse of spiritual information to draw upon when some deeper response is required – quite the opposite. We become the spiritual storehouse, and this new spiritual truth is fully invested in us. We are the walking, talking, evidence of all spiritual truth. We don't dial it up as the need arises – we are it 24/7, it is the new us.

God created humanity with a natural, innate ability to receive spiritual truth on face value. But Adam destroyed that ability and replaced it with a filter that operates like this – 'what do I have to do to make this truth operate in my life'.

So now instead of 'being' the truth of God – we 'do' it.

God has declared who we are. He has declared our new divine nature, our status in His Kingdom, and our condition as righteous and holy. The problem is that we take this information and set about attempting to make it true by our righteous living – *when it is already true.*

Can you see the difference?

When God created humanity He wrote a code into us. It was a spiritual code, just like DNA is our natural code. The code is this; you are the expression of God's best, He dreamed you up, you are the master craftsman's workmanship on His best day ever. He will never, ever regret one single thing that He built into your uniqueness for all of eternity. He loves you so much that He allowed Jesus to suffer and die for you, because He couldn't contemplate His eternity without you in it – *with Him.*

Adam lost the code.

And Jesus gave it back to us. He gave us back our original design, the one that is made out of God's image. God didn't lose it, Adam did. God had it in safe-keeping in Christ, and Jesus has returned us back to our true self.

I don't want this to seem like too much of a circular conversation, one that circles continuously around the human dilemma – but I know from experience that my natural mind rejects this spiritual information, much like my body attempts to reject a virus. My natural mind is so committed to the notion that God cannot express His love to me unless I impress Him with a lovable life, that it attempts to expel anything to the contrary.

My natural mind is not trying to be deliberately difficult; it just can't see that there is a better way.

My natural mind cannot imagine that my spirit is better equipped to direct my life than my soul. It has only ever known soul-direction, it reasons 'if it ain't broke, don't fix it'.

But God did have a much better way in the beginning, so let's leave this circular conversation behind for now and look more closely at this 'better way'.

CHAPTER 14
The Better Way

Psalm 23 says, "He restoreth my *soul*" – what a beautiful turn of phrase from David's famous psalm.

It reminds me of that beautiful hymn, "When peace like a river attendeth my *soul*… it is well, with my soul".

Our soul needs nurturing because life gives it quite a hammering. It yearns for restoration, and to be 'attended by peace'. Our soul seems to cop all that life delivers. It tries its best to figure out how to handle life's challenges, but often finds itself emotionally depleted and experiencing a sense of being overwhelmed. Our soul musters up all of its reserves, and works hard to reason its way through to the best outcome. It applies its most positive attitude, and digs deep to lift itself above the onslaughts of life.

Our soul has been given a task it was not designed for.

Our spirit was set aside by Adam as our internal life-management system, and our soul was promoted to a position it wasn't qualified for – all because Adam believed satan's lie 'you will be like God'. Adam was already like God in every way that mattered, and knowing 'good and evil' was a complication he really didn't need.

So our soul was handed a task that was beyond it – managing good and evil.

Deep down, our soul knows this. It recalls a distant memory of when things were different, and it longs for that time to return. It longs to be restored to its former self.

Our soul remembers a time when it wasn't burdened with the heavy responsibility of producing righteousness; it was a time when it was free to be exactly what it was created to be –expressive, creative, full of vitality, adventurous and even romantic. Our soul is that unique 'us' that was designed to connect with life without the limitations of expectation. It was designed to give expressions to our individual, perfect, unique version of humanity, the one that God gave to us as a gift of love, and then set us free to take hold of this wonderful life with both hands.

Our soul yearns for this self-expression, safe in the knowledge that our spirit holds our true identity and worth, as it revels in its union with God. Our soul and our spirit were designed like a hand in a glove. The life of God in our spirit, found its expression on the earth through a soul that was secure. It was secure in the knowledge that it was the perfect expression of a deep union with the one who is truly perfect. Just like a hand inside a glove, our spirit and soul were designed to operate together in perfect unison, with the hand (spirit) as one with the source of life, and the glove (soul) as the expression of that life.

This perfect expression of humanity was like a dance. Our spirit and our soul performed the most magnificent waltz, moving as one through the beauty of all that life presented. The spirit leading as it rested in the love and life of God, and the soul carried effortlessly along knowing that our spirit knew its way. It was the most beautiful expression of joy the earth has ever seen.

The soul was made for this effortless expression – and it yearns to dance again, leaning-in to the embrace of Jesus – spirit to Spirit.

I remember as a young boy being asked by my mother to watch my little sister while she went outside to hang up the washing – I took the responsibility very seriously, and was so pleased to be relieved of that responsibility when my mum came back inside. I knew deep down that I wasn't designed for it, I was just a little boy, and didn't know how to carry the responsibility of a grown up. I know now that my mum was only out of the house for a few minutes and that she wouldn't leave if there was a danger of something going wrong – but I felt the responsibility none the less.

The human soul is like that little boy, it has been entrusted with a responsibility that it was never designed for, and has to bear that responsibility for a lifetime, not just a few minutes.

> *The human soul doesn't know what to do when something goes wrong.*
> *It is out of place with the heavy responsibilities of life.*
> *It yearns for restoration to its origins, it longs to dance again.*

Our soul is carried aloft by the security and identity which our spirit enjoys, as it rests in and feeds on the life and love of God. Our soul flies over the vagaries of life when it is relieved of the heavy responsibility of constructing its sense of worth. If it knows that it is not carrying the load, then it soars above life's struggles, because its reason and emotions are not the measure of its security. These come from a much higher place all together – the heart of God.

Our soul can only let go when it knows everything is safely held by God.

Remember in Philippians 4:12, Pauls says, "I have learned the secret of being content in any and every situation". He was resting in the truth reported to him by his spirit, not the circumstances experienced by his soul.

Jesus mother, Mary, on learning that she would be the mother of Jesus, expressed this perfect balance in her joyful song, "My *soul* magnifies the Lord, and my *spirit* rejoices in God my saviour". The soul expresses through emotions, thoughts, and deep desires of the heart, all that the spirit knows to be true. Her soul could only magnify the Lord, because her spirit knew God. Without that perfect balance, our soul is left to dance alone, but it doesn't know the steps – *(it was designed to follow not lead)* – and a religion of dead works is its only way forward.

Paul adds to this clarification of soul and spirit as he reflects on Adam in Genesis 2:7 *(NHE)* and Jesus in his present day. The Genesis scripture describes Adam's first breath, "The Lord God formed man from the dust of the ground, and breathed into his nostrils the breath of life; and man became a living soul". This was more than mouth-to-mouth resuscitation; this was the spirit of God awakening Adam to spiritual life.

Then in 1 Corinthians 15:45 *(WEB)* Paul adds, "The first man Adam became a living soul; the last Adam became a life-giving spirit". The last Adam is Jesus; He gives us life by the breath of His Spirit. Our soul lives upon the breath of God, as it allows Jesus to do what He does best – give life. Our spirit rests in this life-source as it revels in its perfect union with Jesus, and our soul joins in too as it allows this life source to lead it in the dance of life.

Our spirit is eternal. It has been in the heart of God forever, and our soul is the expression on earth of our spirit's joy. Once again King David provides helpful clarification in Psalm 139:16 *(NAS)*, "Your eyes have seen my unformed substance; and in your book were written all the days that were ordained for me, when as yet there was not one of them". Even before we had any substance, God's eyes saw our being.

For years, the Christian church didn't make any distinction between spirit and soul, it lumped them together as if the two words were describing the exact same thing. Much as we might call an automobile a car, we might also call a spirit a soul.

This simplistic thinking has robbed us of the depth of our union with God. It has set us apart from Him as the soul attempts to navigate the rapids of life on its own, when all along, our spirit knows that God has all of our days written in His book, *and nothing catches Him by surprise.*

There is a sublime joy in knowing that we were made for such a time as this. Our soul knows, deep down, that it was made for this time in history when the redemption of Jesus would set it back into its origins. When we lift off the heavy burden it has carried for far too long, and allow it to simply enjoy God, our soul cries out, 'this is me, at last I can be who I truly am!' The Westminster Confession says, "The chief purpose of man is to glorify God, and enjoy Him forever". Our soul knows, deep down, that this is true, and it longs for the day of its release.

Yet the only way that our soul can ever have this release is if we grasp the spirit's identity in Christ.

> **Our soul cannot step down
> until we understand what our spirit has stepped up in to.**

Someone has to be in charge, and if we don't recognise our spirit's rightful place 'in Christ' then our soul must remain at the helm indefinitely. Only when our soul understands the sublime condition of our spirit, can it step down, and allow 'walking in the Spirit' to really begin.

There is nothing lacking in the work of Christ. God is not keeping anything from us until some appointed time. The time is now. Our spirit has been called back to its true identity, and now, all of heaven is watching and waiting for the sons of God to be revealed. We are revealed as God's sons when we assume with humility and dignity our true selves – 'Christ in me'.

The only reason we delay is because we are not convinced that the Spirit of Christ 'in us' is able to do as well as our soul has been doing. We are so used to the soul's self-generated righteousness that we can't imagine a life where the Spirit of God 'in us' accomplishes more than we ever could by sheer human zeal and dedication.

That's why Jesus urges us in Matthew 11:28-29 "Come to me, all you who are weary and burdened, and I will give you rest. Take my yoke upon you and learn from me; for I am gentle and humble in heart, and you will find rest for your *souls*". We only find the rest that our soul craves when we let go of the heavy burden of man-generated good works, and take upon ourselves the light yoke of the Spirit of Jesus.

This is the rest that our spirits have entered into, and our souls must follow suit. In fact, Hebrews 4:10 *(BSB)* tells us that unless we enter this spiritual rest, we are being disobedient; "So there remains a Sabbath rest for the people of God. For whoever enters God's rest also rests from his own work, just as God did from His. Let us, therefore, make every effort to enter that rest, so that no one will fall by following the same pattern of disobedience".

The Spirit of God is calling our soul back to this restful union that it was first designed for. It is calling our soul to step back into the role of restfully leaning-in to the finished work of Christ that our spirit knows so well. When we do that, our soul is at last released from the pattern of disobedience.

Our reluctance is generally based on an incorrect understanding of the work that Jesus accomplished on the cross. We tend to think that Jesus died for all our sins up to the moment we received salvation, and then we take over and strive to live a godly life, confessing our sins when we slip-up, and then redoubling our efforts to live right again.

All this thinking does is keep the soul in the driver's seat.

The soul cannot possibly surrender its responsibility to provide a righteous life if we have not grasped that Jesus takes care of both sides of the equation.

> **He provides for our righteousness before we receive salvation,
> and He continues to provide it once we are saved.**

When we correctly understand that Jesus not only paid the price for our sin debt, but also crucified the life that generates that sin, then we can confidently step up into our new identity. There is no more work to do. Our soul is excused from its role, as our spirit leans-in to the righteous, life-giving heart of God.

What a relief!

CHAPTER 15

Too Good to be True

This gospel sounds too good to be true. As I have said before, 'if the gospel of Jesus doesn't seem too good to be true, then it probably isn't the gospel'. The gospel of Jesus is outrageous, it is shocking! Jesus takes us back for free; we don't even need to lift a finger for it.

Overcoming the thought that this gospel is too good to be true is our next challenge. Getting our heads into the space where we accept that our salvation was God's idea, and more than that, that it was 'His desire', takes a major shift. We have become so accustomed to the rule of karma 'you get what you give', that we find it hard to process the notion of an alternative 'we get what we give nothing for'.

This problem is compounded by the fact that our soul finds its identity in doing, we are wired-up by our inheritance from Adam to purchase the commodities of life by human effort, and our salvation is no different.

There is a way out.

The first step is to acknowledge that our right-standing with God is God's gift to us, not our gift to God.

To compare the value of the sacrifice of the King of Glory to our meagre attempts to generate goodness through lifestyle and religion is ludicrous. God doesn't need our contribution to tip the scales.

Then, we need to realise that by ceasing to construct our security with God out of the pleasing lifestyle we offer him, doesn't mean that we stop living decent godly lives – it just means that we don't lean on this lifestyle as playing a part in our sense of security with God. We continue to live well, why wouldn't we? In fact, the motivation to live well gets complicated when we mix-in the spiritual maintenance factor. We are much better at being good when it isn't confused with the role of maintaining our identity, or getting God's approval and attention.

This is where faith comes in. To believe in the ability of the blood of Christ alone as the means of providing our righteousness requires faith. It means we have to conduct a very serious scrutiny of the work that Christ undertook on the cross and determine if it was enough. We need to take ownership of it as an alternative to our previous means of security.

Like trading in a car, we need to give up the old one so that we can possess the new one. When we buy a new car, the dealer doesn't tell us we can drop by anytime and use the old car, it is gone, we will never see it again. And similarly, we need to let go of our old means of shoring up our security with God, and fully embrace the blood of Christ for that purpose.

This is a major crossroad.

It is a completely different road, on an entirely new map. It is setting out on a journey with God that is in the opposite direction to our previous journey, and taking a road we have never explored before. If it doesn't feel this way, then the soul is still trying to maintain control. The mark of this journey is that it barely seems to parallel our old Christian paradigms.

It's easy to get stuck here because some of our religious heritage is so entrenched in our thinking. Take the 10 commandments for instance; this is held up as such a holy and sacred part of our Christian doctrine, yet it belongs in the Old Covenant which Jesus abolished at the cross. Jesus gave us a new way that works better than the old; He gave us His Spirit to lead us, instead old the old way of the law. It's not that God doesn't want us to live upright lives; it's that He gave us an alternative that works much better than religious and lifestyle observances.

We take all of 'the eggs' that we have previously distributed across our many lifestyle and religious practices, and we place them all into Christ. He becomes our complete source of security; he is now the basket in which all of our security is found. If He fails then we are sunk. But He won't fail, because we have scrutinized the work of the cross, and have determined that it is sufficient to completely carry us through.

You might be thinking, "But can't I do both?" The answer is simply, 'You can do what you like', God is already satisfied, so 'doing both' doesn't even enter into His head. He already sees you hidden in the work of Christ.

> *If God is already satisfied*
> *then the only person left in the frame is you –*
> *What is best for you?*

You and I were designed to live in the Spirit. Our original blueprint had us designed as spiritual flying machines, people who are carried aloft by the breath of God, people who lived in the stratosphere of the Kingdom of God. Adam remade us as earthbound doers, people who have constructed their identity out of doing good deeds upon the earth.

If we insist on remaining people of our fallen condition, then God is not going to force us to live in the Spirit. He has given us all that the blood of Christ has achieved and obtained, the choice to walk in it is ours. Yet the hosts of heaven must scratch their heads when they look at the hordes of Christianity – *'they have been given the Spirit but they choose the flesh instead – go figure!'*

The problem with humanity is that in our unredeemed condition, we are soul-directed beings, and that problem is compounded by the fact that the soul has hidden the solution that Christ provided from our view.

The soul says, 'The life I have constructed must be right because it feels so right, and besides, everyone else is operating this way. The majority view is my safe place. I don't feel comfortable going against the stream'.

The spirit says, 'Christ has given me an alternative. It is a narrow road that leads to life, and few find it. I won't limit my 'adventure in the Spirit' to the experience of the masses. I will respond to the gentle and humble heart of Jesus, He can carry me into a life I never before dreamed possible'.

This life is not primarily about changing our circumstances on the earth, that is the secondary outcome of this life. This life is about living abundantly in the midst of the circumstances of life, and then watching them change as we rest in the completed work of Christ. This life begins in our thinking, Proverbs 23:7 *(NKJB)* says, "As a man thinks in his heart, so is he". As we begin to think as people of the Spirit, we discover a lightness of life that is new – circumstances seem to lose their ability to press upon us, because Christ is bearing the load, not us.

We were made for it.

It seems like such an insignificant thing at the start… choosing the righteousness of Christ over our own righteousness as the source of our security. But as we let go and lean-back into the nature of Christ, a remarkable thing begins to happen – 'peace that passes all understanding' becomes our day-to-day reality.

We didn't know it could be like this because the soul had hidden it from us, but now that we have it, we can never live any other way again.

In rounding off this part of the book, I would like to take a look at a unique characteristic of the soul. As I mentioned earlier, the un-regenerated soul gathers its information from the physical evidence. It constructs a view of reality which is entirely made up of the information presented by the physical realm.

Let's look deeper into the soul.

CHAPTER 16
The Soul

It doesn't come as a surprise that the soul looks at our day-to-day circumstances and interprets these as the indicators of our real identity. *It works with what it can see.* It sees our lives from the perspective of the physical realm only, and concludes that this is the sum of our identity. It lacks the ability to see the realities that exist in the spiritual realm, and so all of its conclusions are earth-based.

But there is an even greater dilemma that we face when the soul is in charge – it also interprets the word of God on the basis of the physical evidence. The believer may indeed give a polite nod to the spiritual realities in God's word, but they have not made the leap to elevate them to the position of our primary truth – God's truth remains in subordination to the physical evidence.

So we find ourselves reading the word of God and sub-consciously moving spiritual truths into the realm of physical evidence. We take a truth that the Holy Spirit declares to us and attempt to locate a physical context for it, so that our soul can own it.

Hebrews 11:1 describes the way of the spirit, "Now faith is confidence in what we hope for and assurance about what we do not see". Spiritual truth is accepted without the need for physical evidence to support it, not the other way around.

A statement of clarification about why I am spending so much time distinguishing between the spirit and the soul: We as the human race were re-wired by Adam to come at our understanding of God on the basis of the information we perceive from our human reasoning and five senses. Jesus undid Adam's wiring and re-set us as people who can now live from the much higher reality of the spirit. To do this we need to re-activate a way of thinking which is in stark contrast to

Adam's way, we must choose to re-elevate the unseen truths which God declares about us, to be above and more real than the evidence we see with our natural eyes.

As I said, we give a nod to the existence of the spiritual realm (it's hard not to when it proliferates the word of God), but rather than elevating this to its proper place as the primary reality of our lives, we keep it in subservience to the natural realm. In other words; if we can't find physical evidence to support this spiritual truth, then we sub-consciously file it away as figurative, or future-based.

Let me give you an example from the Garden of Eden:

We take the statement that 'Adam was created in God's image'. Our minds tell us that this could not possibly mean that Adam was created out of the same spiritual substance as God because the physical evidence that we perceive in life is that we ourselves, and humanity at large, is dramatically un-god like. So we take this spiritual statement and find a physical explanation for it that seems more plausible 'Adam looked and acted a bit like God'. *It's not perfect, but at least now we have a concept that we can work with.*

Or perhaps this one:

'God walked with Adam in the cool of the evening'. Our minds tell us that Adam was a physical being just like us, so we construct a physical context for God that suits our broken thinking – 'God and Adam did what physical people do, they walked, and chatted, and met-up for a chinwag at the end of the day'. The fact is, Adam and God shared a perfect spiritual union continuously. This union was beyond the bounds of time and space – it was eternal. And no such physical context was necessary to contain it. Besides, God only walked in the cool of the day after Adam had sinned and stepped out of the realm where they had previously met in continuous, spontaneous fellowship. Adam couldn't be found in the spiritual, so God sought him out in the natural.

Our union with God is minimized when we pull it into the physical realm. That's why Paul came up with such statements as 'you are seated in heavenly places' or 'you are citizens of heaven'. He was trying to pull our thinking out of its habit of going to the natural context to validate the spiritual reality.

He was saying, 'get used to it! You are spiritual'.

Or maybe this one from Hebrews 10:14, "By one sacrifice He has made perfect forever, those who are being made holy". We take a spiritual fact 'we have been made perfect forever by the sacrifice of Jesus' and interpret it through the context observed with our natural eyes – our lives don't appear to be very perfect at all. So we overlay this truth with an explanation that better fits into our logical minds, that we are being made perfect as we submit ourselves to a daily process of crucifying our flesh. We take the most staggering claims of the gospel of Jesus and normalize them into a more believable form. We use the physical evidence to interpret a spiritual truth.

Or this one from 2 Corinthians 5:21, "God made Him who had no sin to be sin for us, so that in Him we might become the righteousness of God". Once again, we look at the evidence on the ground and determine that Paul was using some creative licence. We think; 'Clearly, we are not the righteousness of God right now because the evidence of our imperfections is constantly before us'. We inadvertently look to the physical evidence as the measure of validating the work of Christ, and deduce that Paul was speaking figuratively or positionally, but certainly not literally. So we are robbed of the truth. In pulling the word of God into a physical context where we find it more believable, we are actually negating the power within it to do the very thing for which it was intended – give life. So it remains a theology that we adhere to, rather than a living truth that we rest in.

In effect, our soul is making a very ambitious claim, 'I can do for you all that the spirit claims to do'. It's actually the same claim that caused all our problems back in the garden at the beginning, but now it takes the gospel of Jesus and declares 'I can manage this for you – just leave it with me and I will provide you with a logical explanation for all of the claims of Christ, the main thing is to allow me to remain in charge'.

'I will hold you in the physical realm where your true identity lies, and together we will live-out a hybrid form of Christianity. This hybrid takes the pure sacrifice of Jesus, and mixes in the *obvious* need for a physical explanation, and a manmade expression'. And 'wha-la' out comes modern Christianity.

The physical explanation and human expression are worthless if we have not first lost ourselves in the most improbable revelation ever presented to humanity – that we have been made like God.

The soul convinces us that by commitment and focus we can gradually progress towards the outcomes of the Spirit. However, the Spirit declares that all the outcomes of the cross of Christ became ours in the exact instant that we first believed.

Unfortunately for many, the soul is determined to keep the saving process going, it is what it has done for a very long time.

CHAPTER 17

The Spirit

Let's take a step in the direction of the realm of the spirit, and have a closer look at the outcomes that Jesus gave us in that split second in time when we crossed over from death to life.

In the realm of nature, the outcomes of that event were hardly noticeable. This is because, contrary to what we may have thought, it wasn't primarily about our existence in the realm of nature. Our soul may have done a quick scan of the landscape to see if anything had changed, but probably came to the quick realization that it was business as usual, just within a slightly different cultural context.

Our soul has no idea what actually transpired.

We were re-born as spiritual beings in a flash of time, and yet our soul felt nothing. Maybe a bit of emotional excitement, but certainly not the momentous thing that had just taken place beneath the surface.

We had just re-entered heaven, and our soul missed it.

Our spirit had just been subjected to all of the power of the divine defibrillator and our soul was too preoccupied with physical things to see it. *We really shouldn't look to the soul to determine a spiritual reality.*

In spite of what our soul failed to notice, our spirit has just been transformed.

It was dead to God and alive to satan. Now it is dead to satan and alive to God. This transformation is momentous and far-reaching because it begins in the blink of an eye when we first turn our face back to Jesus. We were citizens of hell, and now we are citizens of heaven. Not citizens of earth who are possibly going to heaven or hell, but people already dwelling in one or the other according to our reception of Christ. In fact, not only do we become citizens of heaven and dwell there with God, He becomes citizens of us and dwells in our hearts. John 17:14, "They are not of this world, any more than I am of this world".

Once our spirit changed address it was subject to the most radical of transformations – enslaved in sin to eternal freedom. We were dead in the mire of sin, now we are alive in the perfect heart of God.

Let's view this thing from God's perspective. After all we are now reunited with Him.

Just think about it, Jesus said in John 14:20, "On that day you will realize that I am in my Father, and you are in me, and I am in you". He is likening our union 'in Him' to His union 'in the Father'. We must take a moment to ponder this. Elsewhere he says that if you have seen me, you have seen the Father. Could Jesus really be saying that the reality of our fusion to Him is no different to the reality of His fusion to the Father? *Why wasn't I told this sooner?*

It changes everything.

It means that I am no longer a leaf tossed in the winds of life, subject to every whim of this sinful world. I am home safe in God, back in my true origins again. I am no longer a spectator of God's glory, watching Him reveal Himself to the world. Never, I am the spectacle, He is revealing His handiwork in me, I am the best He can do (Christ's sacrifice displayed in me), and He is very pleased with the result.

The entire realm of the spirit marvels at this spectacle, yet our soul diminishes it for the lack of physical evidence!

Christ became sin, so that I could become the righteousness of God and be put on display for the entire world to see. Look at what the blood of Christ has done, isn't the righteousness of God such an astonishing display of His love, as it finds its home in me?

This is what the Father sees.

This is what is meant by 1 Samuel 16:7 *(NLT)*, "People judge by outward appearance, but the Lord looks at the heart". God sees all the way past my human imperfections, they are simply the jar of clay that contains my true self. He looks at the real me, and as He does, He sees the perfection of my big brother, Jesus.

> **As far as God is concerned, I no longer exist in any condition
> other than in my union with Jesus.**

He is not tolerating my weaknesses out of regard for Jesus, or even turning a blind eye because I am trying my best – not at all. That person no longer exists in God's reality; I have become one with Jesus. The natural realm doesn't influence God's opinion of me.

There is no situation any longer when I am just little old me. When I enter a room, Jesus enters. When I step into a church service the presence of God arrives. If the worship leader asks the Holy Spirit to be manifest, then I must walk up to the platform – *we are inextricably in it together.* Smith Wigglesworth was once heard to say, 'sometimes God moves me, and sometimes I move God' – and I am beginning to get it – he had grasped that he couldn't shake-off Jesus no matter what he did, Jesus had become his permanent other self.

I know, it sounds a little bit weird, but everything about our union with God defies human logic. We have just grown too familiar with the neatly packaged form of Christianity that our soul organized so we wouldn't feel too conspicuous.

But isn't it better to feel a bit 'out of the square', than to disappear into such a bland, normalized version of Christianity that God doesn't even really need to show up? Paul likened us to strangers and aliens in the world; if it was good enough for Paul then perhaps it should be good enough for us too.

My real home is heaven; God has welcomed me back to His glorious presence. Do I really want to 'fit in' down here just to feel comfortable, when He rescued and transported me to a much better place? Don't get me wrong, I love this life on earth, I love my earthly relationships and activities, I enjoy the beauty of creation and the wonders of nature, but I am discovering that they are not a patch on my true home 'in God'.

> **My soul is slowly catching up with my spirit
> and the glory of God is so superior to the glory of the earth
> that sometimes I find myself longing for His courts just like David.**

In Psalm 90:1 *(NLT)* we read a prayer of Moses, "Lord, through all the generations you have been our home". *Heaven is not our home, God is.*

God doesn't relate to us primarily as residents of planet earth, in His mind we are aliens here, just passing through. As far as God is concerned, we live in Jesus now, He is our true habitation. This is not a neglectful or callous perspective; God is not ignoring our daily needs and earthly concerns. Quite the contrary, by placing us into Jesus He has resolved all of the issues that we will ever face both natural and spiritual. God has placed us into the only environment where we can overcome the issues of the world. We are hidden in the one who overcame the world – Jesus himself.

As Jesus said in John 16:33, "I have told you these things, so that in me you may have peace. In this world you will have trouble. But take heart! I have overcome the world".

In 2 Peter 1:3 *(BSB)* we read, "His divine power has given us everything we need for life and godliness" – Peter went on to be martyred. Did God's divine power run out when Peter needed it most? Certainly not, Peter was already living in Jesus long before martyrdom took him. He had already left the building, and his physical life followed along in due course.

In the spiritual sense we have also left the building. John 5:24 says, "I tell you the truth; whoever hears my word and believes Him who sent me has eternal life and will not be judged *but has crossed over from death to life*". We are citizens of heaven right now just as certainly as Jesus and the angelic hosts are citizens of heaven, we have crossed over, we have graduated, we are home.

Hebrews 10:19 & 22 puts it beautifully, "Therefore, brothers, since we have confidence to enter the Most Holy Place by the blood of Jesus… let us draw near to God in full assurance of faith". The blood of Jesus has achieved the impossible. I have been made so perfect that I can stand before the Holy throne of The Most High God. This is the 'me' that God sees.

And He is so assured that Christ's blood has done the job in me, He is so delighted with new person that stands before His holiness, that He puts me on display for all the world to see. Ephesians 2:10 "For we are God's masterpiece. He has created us anew in Christ Jesus, so we can do the good things He planned for us long ago".

God is not winking at my imperfections out of regard for the sacrifice of Jesus, nor is He congratulating me for doing my best and holding the line despite my poor past record. He simply cannot find any un-holiness in me.

He is not like us; He doesn't see the train wreck of our lives, nor does He relate to us as residents of planet earth. In His eyes we are washed cleaner than snow, and the virtue of Jesus has become our new self.

> *He is not putting the old me on display, but the new me.*
> *He is putting 'Jesus in me' on display to the universe.*

Does this seem like a bit of a stretch to you? If so, dial-down your soul and dial-up your spirit.

Your spirit knows some astonishing things. It sits-in on all the board meetings of heaven. Heaven is a family business; everyone gets a seat on the board. We are all there 'in Christ'. When the Father opens the meeting, there is only one item on the agenda 'the blood of Jesus'. There is no reference to the human drama, no tally of sins, no keeping tabs on who is doing what – everything is swallowed-up in that one overarching divine agenda.

The blood of Jesus has made all things new.

It's quite a short meeting. There is no more to discuss – the blood of Jesus has done its work.

We are like the pearl of great price in Matthew 13:46 *(BSB)*, "Again, the kingdom of heaven is like a merchant in search of fine pearls. When he found one very precious pearl, he went away and sold all he had and bought it". That's what Jesus did; He sold all He had to take possession of me. Such is the value He places on my life.

There is no condescension or patronizing here, Jesus did this for far higher reasons than that – His love for me.

We can focus on the demise of humanity all we like, but in the end, it is not about what we, or Adam, or anyone, did wrong – it is about what Jesus did right. We must get our heads into that place.

> *God is not going over and over the shortcomings of humanity;*
> *He is obsessed with the stunning accomplishments of the blood of Jesus.*
> *And so should we be.*

I know some folk who have turned the worst thing that ever happened to them into a memorial day, they re-live the effects of that event for every day that follows. But wouldn't it be better to turn the best thing that ever happened to us into the day we are obsessed with? It's tough getting over the hardships that life throws at us, but these things cannot define us unless we give them permission. Jesus rescued us from hell and presented us holy before His Father, surely that is more momentous than our worst day.

Our Heavenly Father Himself endured a terrible day when He turned His face away from the one He loves, and allowed Him to bear the sins of the whole world, yet He has lost that terrible event in the joy of our redemption. God is preoccupied with the best thing that ever happened to us, not the worst that we have ever done – and we should be too.

Are you game?

Are you ready to believe in God's goodness as much as He believes in you?

CHAPTER 18

To Agree with God

The highest expression of humanity is not to please God... *but to agree with Him.*

God is not waiting for us to present him with an acceptable lifestyle of worship and service; He is waiting for us to say, **"You were right God, all you have said about me concerning the application of the blood of Christ on, and in me, is correct. From this moment forward, I agree with you. I have become like Jesus. This is my true identity, I repent of (turn away from) my past identity, and embrace the opinion that you now have of me."**

From this moment on, I no longer live, but Christ lives in me. The life I now live in the body, I live by faith in the Son of God, who loved me, and gave Himself for me.

There are two scriptures that pick up this theme of our spiritual knowledge and sight:

1 Corinthians 13:12, "Now I know in part; then *I shall know fully*, even as I am fully known".

1 John 3:2, "Dear friends, now we are children of God, and what we will be has not yet been made known. But we know that when Christ appears, *we shall be like Him*, for we shall see Him as He is".

Both of these scriptures refer to a capacity to perceive our true spiritual condition, our spirits have this capacity now – they are like Jesus and they fully know Him.

Our part is to consciously agree with the knowledge that our spirit has, and to allow it to rise to the surface as our real every day identity.

There are some that would suggest that this approach is 'soft on sin', that it diminishes the scale of the problem and over simplifies the solution.

They would suggest that it takes the sin problem too lightly to suggest that we can live as if it doesn't exist. In the end, it comes down to which voice we choose to listen to – the voice of our soul declaring the visible evidence of humanity's continuing failure to live right, or the voice of our spirit declaring that Christ has made us right already.

In my view, the voice of our spirit takes a harder line on sin than the voice of our soul. Our spirit declares that sin was a problem that was far beyond the capacity of the soul to resolve, and it took a much greater solution to rectify it than our soul could apply to the problem. Our spirit sees the scale of the sin problem and the astounding capacity of the sacrifice of Christ to crush it, and it concludes that it is finished.

> *Our soul believes in US – more than it believes in JESUS.*

Our soul keeps the sin problem in play because its role and identity is dependent on it, when all along the sin problem has been totally destroyed by the power of Christ's blood sacrifice. It is reasonable to conclude then that "the soul is actually much softer on sin than the spirit".

It's important that we get this issue of the soul's need for identity sorted out.

Our soul is designed to find its identity somewhere, God made it that way. Identity in itself is not a bad thing, it is simply the internal opinion we have of ourselves. There are some who find identity in their physical appearance, others in their intellectual or creative capacity, and others in the various causes and social programs they apply themselves to.

When God made Adam, He gave him an identity that was entirely built upon his union with God. His identity came from his spiritual condition. The physical realm was God's gift to him to live in and enjoy, but it played no part in his identity. His identity was entirely wrapped up in the wonderful love and life that he shared with God.

You could say that Adam was made with a non-ego, it never occurred to him to turn the spotlight on to himself because the glory of God was so spectacular.

> *Everything about Adam's union with God*
> *satisfied and validated his need for identity.*

When Adam decided to base his life on his own management of good and evil, rather than his union with God, his sense of identity shifted from the spirit to the soul. It is this shift of identity, from the spirit to the soul which most defines the human problem. Christ came to correct this identity crisis. He came to reinstate our spirit as the source of our identity, and our part is to let Him.

Colossians 3:1-3 puts it beautifully, "Since, then, you have been raised with Christ, set your hearts on things above, where Christ is, seated at the right hand of God. Set your minds on things above, not on earthly things. For you died, and your life is now hidden with Christ in God".

This verse is not telling our soul to be religious and apply itself to the tasks of good living (which would be reinforcing the soul's identity with even more self-generated worth), it is saying that Jesus killed the soul's independence from God, and re-hid its identity in the virtue of Christ.

Can you see the issue here?
The soul attempts to perpetuate the very same approach that Adam did all those years ago, when he walked away from God's freely given life.

In John 6:57 Jesus tells us, "Just as the living Father sent me and I live because of the Father, so the one who feeds on me will live because of me". Jesus is telling us to feed on Him, in the same way that Adam had spiritual life as long as he fed on the Tree of Life. Jesus is the Tree of Life – our spiritual vitality comes from feeding on Him, not our own self-made identity.

The reason why the alternative tree is called 'The Tree of the Knowledge of Good and Evil' is because it causes us to lift our eyes off the free gift of life, which comes from the Tree of Life, and fix them on our own good or evil behaviour. In other words, the problem is not necessarily that we do evil, but that we construct our identity out of 'what we do' – *good or evil.*

This is where the whole thing becomes a bit sinister; satan doesn't care if we do good things, as long as we look to them for our identity and security, and not the life of Christ. Satan has no problem with someone being fully absorbed in any one of the many good social causes, religious activities and mission outreaches on offer. He doesn't even care if we give our bodies to be burned for the sake of injustice or oppression. Just as long as we don't lift our eyes off these things and fix them on Jesus for our entire sense of identity and worth.

Let me say that again. Good, bad or indifferent – satan doesn't care. He is content just so long as we are distracted from Jesus by anything. He just doesn't want us to grasp that if we rest in Jesus he is finished. Because then works of life overflow from us like a fountain, all by themselves.

The soul has constructed a clever copy of the heart of Jesus. It has developed a system that appears to produce exactly the same things that Jesus would if He was on the earth – acts of kindness, giving to the poor, and so on. Sadly we have become so defined by these activities, that they are now our primary expression of Christianity, rather than faith in Jesus.

And so we 'do' Christianity without actually 'knowing' Christ.

And in doing so, we inadvertently allow satan ground. The thing satan wants most is to deny Jesus His inheritance – *us*. He has been roundly defeated on the cross in the battle for our eternity, but he continues with his guerrilla warfare hoping to land some injury to Christ. And the only way he can do that is to get us to keep our eyes fixed on ourselves, and not on Jesus. Satan knows he is beaten, the whole spiritual realm see him as a pathetic joke. The only pleasure he has left is to delay our participation in the work of the cross. This is all he has left. And his tool is to constantly turn our attention back to ourselves instead of on to Christ. Just like he did with Adam in the beginning.

CHAPTER 19

Freedom

Psalm 33:12 *(BSB)* says, "Blessed is the nation whose God is the Lord, The people whom He has chosen for His own inheritance". God's inheritance works both ways – He inherits us and we inherit Him. This is the whole point of the cross of Christ – that we be brought back into our original union with God. Jesus has done His part, our release from the old ways of the flesh has been fully enacted, and we *are* free. Now it is up to us to walk in that freedom.

Paul said in Galatians 5:1, "It is for freedom that Christ has set us free. Stand firm, then, and do not let yourselves be burdened again by a yoke of slavery". Christ has set us free so we can live by the spirit, not by being enslaved to the rules. He can't force us to live as free people, all He can do is throw open the prison gates and invite us to walk out.

We have spent a long time in captivity; it is all we have known for millennia. It takes courage to step out into freedom when all we have ever known is the yolk of slavery.

This is not only a freedom from our past bondage to sin, but also a freedom to our new identity in Christ. My experience is that we Christians are more comfortable accepting the 'from' part, and less comfortable accepting the 'to' part. If we don't though, Christ's work is only partly received. Paul makes it quite clear 'it is *for* freedom that we have been set free'. It is not for service, or worship or prayer, but freedom. These others are all the overflow of the primary reason Jesus came. We must discover our freedom first, before any response to God makes sense, else we define ourselves by our response to God, instead of His gift of life.

God doesn't have as big a problem with our freedom as we do. In fact he doesn't have a problem at all – *it is His idea.*

Imagine there is a knock on the door, you go to answer it and Jesus is there. He says to you, "I want you to stop doing everything that's motivated by 'doing the right thing', and then I want you to stop repenting every time you do something wrong. Then, I want you to stop trying to set a good example all the time, and finally (here is the big one), I want you to stop praying for things to change, improve, get fixed, and especially stop praying for my presence. I want you to do this for one year. Don't worry; I will take care of everything in your absence."

"During that year I want you to do just one thing; I want you to discover the meaning of the scripture 'It is for freedom that you have been set free'."

"At the end of that year you are free to take up any of the things that I have asked you to stop. As long as they do not contradict the things you have learned about freedom."

Could you do it?

Or do you have too much invested in a form of Christianity, which functions better through activity, and defines itself through 'our response', rather than freedom to rest in Christ?

In back of this scenario is the notion that it is only when we have a deep revelation 'that we are free to do nothing', and finally learn how to rest in the presence of Christ within, that we can begin to enjoy the reality of His spirit working through us. Paul said in Colossians 1:29 *(BSB)*, "To this end I labour, striving with all His energy working powerfully within me". It's not Paul that produces the results, it's 'Jesus in him' which produces the necessary spiritual vitality to achieve the results. We can't partake in that source of energy without grasping the reality of Christ within.

While we are constantly striving to 'do the right thing', we are distracted from the fact that Christ has done the right thing for us.

While we are always repenting of our sins, we miss sight of the fact that God has hidden all our sins in the sea of His forgetfulness – past, present and future.

While we are focussed on always 'setting a good example', we are more inclined towards bringing change through our own lifestyle, than through the blood of Jesus.

While we are absorbed in praying that God would change or resolve things, we forget that at the cross we were already given everything we need for life and godliness.

And asking Jesus to be present is a bit rude really, when He promised He will never leave us or forsake us.

These are all simple things that we habitually do every day. Could we cope for a year without doing them, knowing that our security is established in God's love, and not in 'ticking the boxes'?

My intention here is not to actually stop us from doing anything, but rather to discover that there is another way to live than the way we are accustomed to. It's a way that achieves so much more than the old system of obligation and effort, because it takes place as the *overflow* rather than the *objective*. Works of life bubble up out of us as we take the time to discover the magnificence of our salvation. *They are the overflow, we can't stop them.*

The 'Holy Spirit in us' achieves them, not us. We can only stop this flow by swinging our focus back on to ourselves again. I have said a few times already, and I will say it again, I am not advocating idleness or indulgent living, but living from a difference source of life, the vitality of 'Christ in me' (trusting Jesus to do it).

> *As I said earlier – 'it takes courage to step out into freedom'.*

It can seem quite reckless when we hear this for the first time. However, our concerns can hold us back from such a superior way of living that it makes the old way look like kindergarten. This is the way we were initially created to live. It is the image of 'God in us', which Christ returned us to when He broke the curse of Adam's way.

Jesus Himself articulated this way to live so clearly in John 5:19, "The Son can do nothing by Himself; He can only do what He sees His Father doing, because whatever the Father does the Son also does". Further on in John 14:10 *(NLT)* we also read, "The words I speak are not my own, but my Father who lives in me does His work through me".

This is the divine principle. Life comes from God, through Jesus, and into us. Without this flow of divine energy, everything we do is self-generated human effort. There is nothing wrong with human effort, it just doesn't have any relevance in the spiritual realm – for that, we need the life of Christ.

This is the myth that humanity at large has carried over from Adam – that God is impressed or moved by what we do. In actual fact, He is only moved and impressed by our faith in what Christ has done. The things we do that spring from our legacy from Adam may indeed have an earthly impact, and there is nothing wrong with that, but don't mistake that earthly outcome as a spiritual accomplishment.

> **Jesus sidelined works, and replaced it with faith.**

Adam did not leave us equipped to live by faith, we have to re-learn this ancient way of living.

Paul said in Romans 14:23 *(YLT)*, "All that is not of faith is sin". He was separating our thinking into two categories – Adam's way (sin) and Christ's way (faith). There is no third alternative; it is either faith or sin.

For much of my life, I thought there was a third way, a kind of middle road. Not being stuck in Adam's rut, but also not embarking on the risky adventure of faith. In reality, it was Adam's way all along; I just thought it was different because I was conscientiously attempting to be a good Christian.

I guess that's the nub of it; Adam was just as serious about doing the right thing as I was, it's just that he separated us all from the only chance we had of actually doing it.

> **Only right believing, can lead to right living.**

CHAPTER 20

Seeing and Knowing

Faith is not what we do; it is what we see (with the eyes of our heart).

If we can see the stunning accomplishments of the cross, then having faith is easy. However, if we are depending on our own spiritual guts and determination then it is exhausting.

Faith comes down to just this one thing; the ability to see who and what we are in Christ. If we don't have the ability to see that, then our attempts to generate faith are nothing more than wishful thinking clothed in human effort.

The thinking of Adam has left us with a somewhat distorted view of faith. We think it is a combination of determination and boldness which we apply to a stubborn object to get it to move – 'faith can move mountains', that sort of thing. The problem here is that we continue to perpetuate the mindset of Adam by attempting to generate this capacity from within ourselves.

In fact, faith has got very little to do with us and everything to do with Jesus. Our only part is to see the accomplishments of the cross with clarity, and place ourselves into those accomplishments. So, instead of faith being about determination and boldness, it is actually about knowledge and sight.

The 'thinking of Adam' attempted to effect change by digging deep into our human resources and stirring up a self-generated response. But before Adam lost his spiritual sight, no such process was required. He simply lived out that which he knew to be true by virtue of his union with God. He didn't have to manufacture anything; his only part was to live-in that which he knew to be true.

> *Adam broke our faith instinct,*
> *and replaced it with a human copy of his own design.*

Jesus has returned to us the same faith instinct that Adam was created with. It is a part of the born again package. We may not have a very focussed awareness of this instinct, but it is there nonetheless, awaiting our participation by leaning back into the new nature that Jesus gave us.

This is the adventure of 'life in the spirit'. We are fully loaded spiritual beings, just like Adam was at the beginning, and our true nature is waiting just beneath the surface for us to embrace.

Once we have accepted that Jesus did indeed provide us with a new nature, the journey of living in that new nature lays ahead. It is our true self, and it waits within us as we slowly learn the un-forced rhythms of the Spirit.

This is not merely theology which we embrace intellectually and emotionally. It is a person, His name is Jesus, and He has joined Himself to us in the most perfect union.

My wife has become part of me, and I of her, we are one flesh. Similarly, Jesus has become part of me and I of Him, we are one spirit. 1 Corinthians 6:17 *(BSB)* puts it quite clearly, "But he who unites himself with the Lord is one with Him in spirit".

Both of these unions are lived in instinctively, rather than intellectually. My knowledge of my wife is not like an operating manual which I refer to when I need to know what to do next. I know my wife, and I know how our relationship works. So we interact toward each other, and our environment at large, from this innate knowledge.

Hebrews 8:11 describes this knowledge beautifully, "No longer will they teach their neighbour, or say to one another, 'Know the Lord,' because they will all know me, from the least of them to the greatest". We can 'know' Jesus in us, in the same way we know our life partner. In fact; Jesus is also our life partner, just in another realm. This is not theology or intellectual knowledge; it is a profound and deep knowing of the heart.

For most of my life, I attempted to apprehend the realities of my new nature by the means of my intellect and emotions (the servants of my old nature). I wanted to *feel* God's presence, and *sense* Him on an emotional level. In effect, I was trying to get my soul to accomplish something that it wasn't cut out for. This instinct is more akin to a child jumping off the kitchen table into her daddy's arms – there is no intellectual process involved, it is simply a deep trust that comes from knowing her daddy loves her.

In the same way, I have had to begin re-learning a trust which is not intellectually based (because my intellect can only view sensory information and respond accordingly), and entrust myself into something much higher, yet invisible. Like the deep trust of the little girl jumping into her daddy's arms, I have had to re-learn how to *deeply* trust God. My intellect says, 'hold back, wait for more evidence', my heart says, 'let go, all the evidence you need was demonstrated on the cross'.

> *It is a turning point, intellect v. heart.*

That's not to say we cease to use our intellect as we walk-out our lives, but rather, that our intellect is placed in to submission to our 'inner knowing'. Our intellect is God's gift to us to help us navigate our way in the physical realm, but it cannot see or understand the things of the Spirit.

1 Corinthians 2:14 *(NKJV)* clarifies this, "But the natural man receives not the things of the Spirit of God for they are foolishness to him; neither can he know them, because they are spiritually discerned".

The natural man has a different instinct. He attempts to generate from within the outcomes that are produced naturally by the Spirit. He can't discern spiritual things, so he engages his personal abilities instead. Such things as boldness, tenacity, intensity and zeal are the natural man's instincts which he calls into action when he thinks faith is required.

But these are not faith. They are merely human behaviour that is observable in the natural realm which has the appearance of faith. Real faith may not contain a physically demonstrative expression at all. It is quite likely to pay scant regard to any outward human expression, because it knows that faith is connected to Christ's demonstration, not ours.

> *Living a life of faith is not about personality or emotion;*
> *it's about what we know.*

In the end, the only difference between Adam and us is that (as a man created in God's image) he never knew any other way to live – whereas we have the established thought patterns of many generations to overcome.

So, did Adam exercise faith?

Not in the same way that modern Christianity views faith. Adam rested in confidence that God could be counted upon. But, unlike us, he had no physical evidence to the contrary. All he did was embrace the most obvious fact in the universe – God loved him and that love provided everything he needed for his security and identity. He didn't have to muster up faith from his own resources until he stepped out of his God/man union.

Did Jesus exercise faith?

Again, not in the same way that modern Christianity views faith. Jesus made it clear all through the book of John that He only did what He could see His Father doing. He knew His Father's love and that love provided everything He needed for His security and identity. He exercised faith in what He could see with His spiritual sight.

Our problem is that we attempt to generate faith without that spiritual sight. In other words, we attempt to create something in opposition to the physical reality, without the spiritual sight to back it up. If we are to attempt to effect the natural realm by exerting faith, then we must be able to see that the result already exists within the work of Christ. God does not reward our self-generated faith by giving us a supernatural outcome; He responds to us as we see the efficacy of the blood of Christ, and place our unwavering confidence in it.

**God responds to our faith in Jesus,
not our faith in our own religious activities.**

That's what trips us up. Adam left us with an in built nature that attempts to provide the solution to our needs by presenting God with a lifestyle of good works and religious activity. We take works of the flesh and re-label them as works of the Spirit, and then hope for a divine outcome. But they were never actually divine works, just fleshy activities that we did in the name of faith.

This truly is the sinister thing about the soul-based perspective we inherited from Adam. Not only does it attempt to generate spiritual life through the means of the flesh, but having done so, it also reports back that these dead works are actually pleasing to God. It is a self-perpetuating cycle that can only be broken as we tear our eyes away from human effort, and fix them squarely on the accomplishments of the cross of Christ.

Jesus returned to us the ability to do this. We each have latent within us the capacity to walk out our days on planet earth as Jesus did, as explained in John 14:12, "I tell you the truth, anyone who believes in me will do the same works I have done, and even greater works, because I am going to be with the Father".

We will do even greater things than He did if we have faith in Jesus. Why? Because we drum up a human response? No, because Jesus went back to the Father as our personal representative.

CHAPTER 21
Uncertainty

Uncertainty is one of the hallmarks of the fallen human condition. We are uncertain about our salvation, uncertain about whether our prayers and our faith are achieving anything, and uncertain if we are in a 'good place' with God. All in all, our assurance of salvation is weak.

This uncertainty is anchored in the notion that our place with God, and His response to us, is directly proportional to whether we are living a life that pleases Him.

Uncertainty was not even on the screen for Adam before he sinned, and it never crossed Jesus mind even for a minute. It is a post-sin phenomenon that came into existence when Adam decided to depend on himself.

Uncertainty is a self-based characteristic which we have overlaid on to our relationship with God. We are uncertain if we are measuring up, and consequently, we are uncertain if God is okay with us.

> *Uncertainty is the characteristic of fallen humanity*
> *that satan takes the most pleasure in.*

We were designed, and subsequently reborn, for a life of rock-solid assurance in God. In 1 John 3:21 we read, "Dear friends, if our hearts do not condemn us, we have confidence before God and receive from Him anything we ask". Our soul tries to get our heart to condemn us, but then the scripture continues, "…because we obey His commands and do what pleases Him. And this is His command: to believe in the name of His Son, Jesus Christ".

This scripture is qualified for us simply by believing in Jesus. It is the only thing necessary to gain confidence before God that we are 'not condemned'.

Jesus gives us back our certainty when we are reborn. He has returned to the Father, and our spirit is with Him there. From this place of life, love and favour we are able to live out our days with absolute certainty in God.

As I have said before, we must see the accomplishments of the cross of Christ with absolute clarity for this kind of faith to operate in our lives. Certainty is founded on what Christ has done, not on what we do.

If our self-doubt causes us to be preoccupied with our own spiritual activities, then we cannot gain a clear focus on Christ's spiritual activity – that's why we are encouraged in the book of Hebrews to "fix our eyes on Jesus, the author and perfector of our faith". Our faith is perfected (made certain) by locking-on to the outcomes of the cross of Christ.

In many respects, the Christian community at large often engages in exactly the same approach as the new age community and the eastern religions. We attempt to generate faith through positive thinking, visualizing and connecting ourselves to our internal energy – only we label it in Christian terms. Faith is only produced by a clear view of Christ and His work; it is never the product of our self-generated effort and positive self-talk.

When we can see the astounding accomplishments of the cross of Christ, and who we have become as a result, all self-help books, methods and principles for engaging God, and well-worn Christian rhetoric and language, become obsolete. We find that we have already arrived at the place that these books and systems speculated about; our search is over – because we are found in Christ.

We Christians are the most remarkable people on the planet. Our journey starts at the finishing line. As soon as we look to Jesus and say "I'm in", we arrive at the ultimate destination. All that remains is the adventure of 'life in the spirit' while we remain on earth. And when we die, our eternal love union with our heavenly Father continues forever. John 5:24 says, "We have crossed over from death to life" – not we *hope* to cross over, or *we may* if we hang in, but *we have*. Our lives on earth are as assuredly lived out in the presence of God, as Jesus is seated there right now. We are in Him, and He is in the Father.

That's why faith is not hard for the reborn Christian. We are already seated at the heavenly banquet with our big brother Jesus, and under the loving gaze of our heavenly Father. Our environment is laden with all the goodness and mercy of God, our cup overflows, and faith is the spontaneous outcome of our life in the abundance of God.

If we can't see this, then I would suggest it is useless to try and manufacture it by pumped up self-effort. For too long, Christians have been trying to prise open the fingers of God through our spiritual push-ups, as though He is reluctant to part with His blessings, favour and love.

> ***What a relief, to at last discover that His hands lay open,
> and we are resting there.***

What a breakthrough to admit our helplessness, and lean in to His strength.

One of the thoughts that might cross our minds is that our relationship with God is a partnership. God does His bit, and I do my bit, and between us both the job gets done. We accept that Christ brokered our release from sin on the cross, but then we add an additional ingredient (human participation) as part of the process necessary to see the blessings of God appear in our lives.

This thinking takes us all the way back to that place of uncertainty.

We wonder if we are doing enough, we wonder if it is God's will, we wonder if God is teaching us something, or maybe even disciplining us. We wonder if there is some trigger to the release of God's favour and blessing that we have missed. And the cycle continues, until we lift our eyes off ourselves, and fix them on Christ alone.

"What about faith?" you may be thinking, "isn't that a response that we need to make?"

As I said earlier, faith bubbles up out of us spontaneously as we see the magnificence of our salvation. It is not an action we take, but simply our ability to see a spiritual fact.

I do not have to exercise faith to operate this computer keyboard. I can see it, so I simply enjoy making use of it. Similarly, faith sees a fact, and simply steps in to it. I also have a pencil on my desk, I can use it instead of my computer if I so choose. It's up to me whether I make use of the superior option. But once my eyes have locked-on to the computer keyboard, the pencil becomes obsolete.

And the same thinking applies to the notion that God requires us to make a response. In the past, I could only see my religious participation, but when my eyes locked-on to the finished work of Jesus, the superior way rendered the old way obsolete. All I 'do' is step into the life of Christ.

Walking in the Spirit is the superior way. Walking in the flesh appeals to our soul-man, but it is so inferior to our real design. The angels in heaven must look on in stupefied wonder when they observe us insisting on adding to the work of Christ, *'they have been given the Spirit of Jesus, but they belittle it by adding works of the flesh?'*

In general terms, we don't rest in the work of Christ, because we don't have a clear view of what He accomplished. We have a scaled down view which appears to require the response of man to activate it.

***God requires no response,
but that we believe what we see with our spiritual eyes.***

Jesus made this quite clear in John 6:28-29, "Then they asked Him 'what must we do to do the works God requires?' Jesus answered, 'The work of God is this: to believe in the one He has sent'."

By nature we are most secure when we are doing our part, because 'simply believing' just doesn't seem like enough. Our soul-man can't process the concept of believing, because it looks for evidence in the wrong place – in natural events. Our spirit-man knows better, and rests secure in the knowledge that Christ's death on the cross is all the evidence it needs, Christ has done it all.

The only way forward is that our soul-man must submit to the instruction of our spirit-man.

CHAPTER 22
Walking in the Spirit

We have been asking the biggest question, and have arrived at a fork in the road. We can continue on the course we have always known, the familiar, predictable way, or, we can embark on a new course, one that is entirely different to the one we have always known.

The superior way is known as 'walking in the Spirit'.

Walking in the Spirit is not an add-on.

It is not a matter of kicking-in to a more focussed way of living as the need arises, much as an athlete might operate differently to his normal everyday life, when he is in training for a marathon.

Walking in the Spirit is an entirely new existence; we do not step into this existence as the need arises because of extenuating circumstances. It is the new atmosphere we live in every moment of every day.

My old flesh nature was convinced that I could walk in the spirit, if, and when, a more focused form of Christianity was required, that it was a more resolute way that I engaged, when my everyday way of life was not up to the task.

By now you can see that this was my soul-man attempting to rationalize a spiritual truth. Without a thorough renewing, our soul-man will always look for a man-generated response to activate a spiritual truth.

In reality, my spirit walks 'in the spirit' continually, and my soul needs to be retrained. It needs to get with the program… the one my spirit is in as it rests in the life of Christ. By nature, my soul tries to retrain my spirit, but it must yield control, and allow the wonder of Christ to take over.

***As my soul lets go of control a wonderful thing begins to happen;
the thing my soul longed for all along begins to happen all by itself.***

My soul always wanted to know the presence and power of God; it just didn't know how to rest in the work of Christ. Now at last it can enjoy life as it was originally designed to – receiving the goodness of God as the free gift it always was, without the need for human behaviour to qualify for it.

But even more than that, now it can rediscover its own true identity.

The soul of man is not bad; it just wasn't designed to produce righteousness. Once the obligation to self-generate righteousness is lifted off the soul, it can begin to discover the extravagance of God's design. It can learn how to walk as the object of God's love.

Let's retrace our steps and clarify the soul's problem before moving on:

The soul of man usurped the role that God designed for the spirit. Adam decided to step out of the union that his spirit enjoyed with God. In the place of this 'union of spirits', he set-up a man generated alternative. This alternative looked to the soul to produce *(from its own resources)* that which the spirit received for free, from its union with God.

The soul of man is the unique combination of intellect, emotions, personality and other personal characteristics which give a person their individuality. These, collectively, are the means by which the soul interacts with the natural environment. They are not however the means by which God designed the soul to construct its identity. Its identity was intended to be the overflow of something much higher than humanity's unique individuality – it was a flow of the love and life that filled our spirit directly from the heart of God.

The spirit of man does not operate on the same level as the soul. It is Spirit-to-spirit (God – to the spirit of man), and it derives all of its identity from this spiritual bond. In other words, the spirit of man has such a complete union with the Spirit of God, that the spirit of man actually takes on God's unique characteristics and identity.

God's design was that the soul of man would live in the natural realm as one hidden in the spirit's identity. The soul of man was not intended to self-generate its identity from its unique characteristics and lifestyle, but to lose itself in the spirit's identity in God.

The soul of man has now been released from the burden of self-generating its identity, and it is at last free to rediscover its true identity, as it restfully leans in to the indwelling Christ.

At the start, Adam had no problem here. He just naturally fed on 'the Tree of Life' to sustain his spiritual vitality. We, however, have to re-learn this ancient ability. We have to re-learn how to feed on Christ for our spiritual sustenance. John 6:57 says, "Just as the living Father sent me and I live because of the Father, so the one who feeds on me will live because of me".

As we feed on Christ, our true identity rises to the surface.

As we feed on Christ, we pick up where Adam left off when he chose independence in favour of union, and the nature of Christ becomes our identity all over again.

We know that our spirit shares in the identity of Christ, and now, also, our soul is able to hide itself in our spirit's identity. *So, what then of all the personal characteristics that are present in our soul? Are they relevant and useful?*

These personal characteristics are now free to express the soul's identity in Christ.

God has set us free to live our lives in response to our unique, individual design, without this individual expression of life being constrained into God's acceptance of us. God accepts us because of who He is, not what we do – and this freedom brings out the best in us.

For instance, if the person leans towards a more creative personality, then creative qualities are released to express the creative vitality of Christ within. God does not constrain us within His pre-determined plan, but releases us to 'live large' with His Spirit within us, energizing us to live great lives. The 'best person we can be' is not the person who is constrained by obligation and responsibilities, but the person who is joyfully carried aloft by the indwelling Spirit of God.

The soul expresses in the natural realm the beauty and wonder of the spiritual realm, which is found in our spirit's continual union with God. This is the human soul in all its magnificence and splendour. It spontaneously lives out the unforced reality of the Kingdom of God in its own unique way.

When our spirit and our soul joyfully express the extraordinary wonder of God, it is like two people singing in perfect harmony. The realm of the Spirit and the realm of nature, each reflecting the glory of God together, just as they were always intended to.

It's interesting that the Westminster Confession describes the chief purpose of man is 'to love God and enjoy Him forever' – yet it not something that we find easy, preferring instead to serve him.

The soul's compulsion to define itself by service rather than sonship is a complete departure from its original design, and the Christian's chief purpose is to rediscover the ancient way. This ancient way is the way that pleases God.

> *Our soul wants to please God through good works,*
> *but God designed us to please Him*
> *by losing ourselves in His unconditional love.*

CHAPTER 23
The True Me

When we lose ourselves in God's unconditional love, our individual characteristics begin to express God in our own unique way. It is the blissful marriage of humanity and divinity, dancing through life in effortless movement – the spirit leading, and the soul leaning-in to the spirit's gentle touch.

Perfection.

As the soul of man embraces the unconditional love of God, it becomes the most radiant display of God's creative work. God made man in His own image, and then filled us with His glory so that we can display Him to all the universe.

We are God's opus – His best work. Humanity is the symphony of the heart of God, each one of us displaying our unique interpretation of the Spirit's presence in us, each hearing the heartbeat of God in our own original way, improvising our individual harmony over the beautiful melody of God's unconditional love.

This is humanity as God created it.

Individuality is celebrated as it wells up from grateful hearts – not competing with God for His glory, but sharing in it as the bountiful overflow of God's heart. Individuality at last makes sense. It is the diversity of the vastness of God displayed in human form, the full spectrum of humanity expressing the splendour of God.

And this is worship too.

As we gaze upon the stunning spectacle of God, our hearts are caught up in a spontaneous outpouring of joy. *We don't 'do' worship*, it simply can't be held in as we revel in the magnificence of a union that originates in God's heart, and returns to His heart. He fills us with himself, and His presence in us reflects His perfection right back into His own face.

God is pleased with us when we let Him be Himself. When we stop trying to please Him, and allow ourselves to become 'His pleasure' in us – then we become the expression of divinity completely at home in humanity. Jesus is God's pleasure, He is the one of whom God said 'this is my beloved Son in whom I am well pleased'. And now Jesus lives in us, the pleasure of God is our new identity, and to live within that pleasure is our highest calling.

The soul of man hungers and thirsts for God's pleasure. Even humanity's original habitation, the Garden of Eden, means 'pleasure garden'. Adam enjoyed the pleasure of God without the need for any personal input. It was the trick of satan that made Adam attempt to access that pleasure through his own means. Yet, it demonstrates our original design. We were created to be the objects of God's pleasure, and this pleasure is automatically ours as we rest in Jesus, and allow His love and life to flow freely through us.

I guess you could say that God takes pleasure in Himself, though not in a human-like egotistical way. God perceives His glory and greatness in the way it should be perceived, because it is the truth. And we are the objects of His pleasure because we are hidden in Him, as Colossians 3:3 says, "Your life is now hidden with Christ in God".

As a result, our soul has a remarkable foundation upon which it can construct a great life. This foundation is that we are hidden in God's goodness and glory. We are the objects of His pleasure and love without even lifting a finger to make it so. 2 Peter 1:3 *(BSB)* says, "His divine power has given us everything we need for life and godliness".

As our soul lets go of the obligation to self-generate righteousness and leans-in to God's divine power and pleasure, it begins to effortlessly partake in the very thing it was striving for. It begins to enjoy life and godliness in the way it was designed to – through restful faith.

There is a flourishing that takes place, a vibrancy. We feel like we were created for such a time as this because we are finally living according to our original design.

> ***The difference between 'doing good' to secure our relationship with God, and 'doing good' because our relationship with God is secure, is paramount.***

The first is a daily grind of trying to 'measure-up' or 'get God involved', the second an effortless walk in the Spirit. Our true design 'in God's image' is only able to operate through the latter of these options; otherwise, we are opting for the inferior model developed by Adam.

But what would such a 'walk in the Spirit' look like in real time, how would it play out in my daily life?

Knowing that we are the objects of God's pleasure without even lifting a finger, propels us to be the best possible version of ourselves. Paul says, "It is for freedom that you have been set free", and the freedom of living in God's pleasure causes our best selves to surface. Our old nature fears freedom because it anticipates unrestrained self-indulgence, but in reality the opposite is true. The beauty of 'no-condemnation' means that we can begin living well for all the right reasons, because we were made for it.

God doesn't regret his original design just because Adam took humanity on his mad experiment for a few millennia. God is still committed to the original, in spite of Adam's diversion. *He got it right the first time,* and He wants us to rediscover the wonder of His original idea. That's why Jesus came, that we might have life *(all over again).*

Our soul is free again to be itself.

CHAPTER 24
A New Way to Live

The original defining characteristic of the soul is that it was free. Adam enslaved the soul of humanity in an existence of perpetual obligation to the Tree of the Knowledge of Good and Evil. We were stuck in a cycle of maintaining our sense of worth through good works. Jesus set us free again, and gave us life in abundance. It is like a brave new world that Adam's legacy kept us from, and now we are free again to rediscover it, just like Adam did at first when God breathed life into him.

In Genesis 2:7 we read, "The Lord formed the man from the dust of the ground and breathed into His nostrils the breath of life, and the man became a living being".

Imagine that moment; Adam opened his eyes for the first time and breathed his first breath, and the magnificence of God's creation filled his senses. This world of God's abundance beckoned him to the adventure of life in the pleasure of God.

He opened his eyes and the heart of God was on display before him.

There was no checklist to satisfy before embarking on this life in God's pleasure; it was a gift that God had prepared in advance, freely given to Adam, simply because God loved him. No strings attached – just life in abundance. God being God, and man being man – life as God designed it.

There were two things happening here. Adam's spirit was living in the creator, and Adam's soul was expressing that life in the creation. This was perfection. Man living in two realms at the same time seamlessly. I doubt Adam was even aware of the difference between the spiritual and physical realms, such was the brilliance of God's creative work. He simply lived in God and loved life.

It worked like this; Adam's spirit lived in God – it was a beautiful union of hearts. It was so complete that Adam automatically participated in the divine nature of God. Adam didn't have to do anything to partake in God's nature but to simply rest in the fact that God was good, and that He loved him. This was all it took for the essence of God's being, to be the essence of Adam's being.

From this sublime union flowed the abundance of God's heart. Adam's spirit was filled with the vitality of God, and his soul lived out this vitality in the natural realm. It was like a channel of God's love and life that flowed from God's heart into Adam's spirit, and out through Adam's soul. It never diminished or ran out, because all Adam had to do was let God be God, and revel in the pleasure of God's nature.

Even though this is the way God made us, it is now the most foreign way for us to live.

> **We are like Adam was at the very beginning,**
> **we have been reborn to live in both realms seamlessly,**
> **the realm of the spirit and the realm of nature, in perfect harmony.**

We have so much relearning to do to take hold of our true design again.

Paul points the way in the first chapter of Ephesians, it is a chapter that shines light on the amazing union we have with God, and how this union plays out in our daily lives here on earth.

In verse 3 and 4 he sets the stage, "Praise be to the God and Father of our Lord Jesus Christ, who has blessed us in the heavenly realms with every spiritual blessing in Christ. For He chose us 'in Him' before the creation of the world to be holy and blameless in His sight".

We are blessed in the heavenly realms with every spiritual blessing in Christ. That means that our spirit is back where it all began. We have the whole package that Adam started with; the banquet of God's love in the heavenly realms is laid out before us. We were chosen 'in Christ' – that means that God's pleasure rested on Jesus, and we are also recipients of it because we are 'in Christ'. It is our divine design. We are in Christ and a life 'in the spirit' results – our soul living out what our spirit declares from the realm of the spirit.

Jesus was not only a spiritual being; He too had a soul like us. Matthew 26:38 "Then He said to them, "My *soul* is deeply grieved, even to the point of death. Remain here and stay awake with me." And in 1 John 4:17, "as Christ was in this world, so are we". Jesus modelled for us the operation of the soul. He clearly had a soul just like us, and His soul had human characteristics and emotions just like us. And Jesus demonstrated for us how a soul that is not constrained by sin lives.

For many years, I thought Jesus was modelling a lifestyle for the flesh part of humanity, that He was giving us an example of how we should lead a life of service, humility, sacrifice and love. But the more I think about it, the more I see that He was primarily giving us a model of how to live in the spirit. He was showing us how to draw life from His Father.

Jesus said in John 6:63, "The Spirit gives life, the flesh counts for nothing", yet we have made a religion out of activating the flesh, training it to copy Jesus, instead of teaching it how to draw life from the Spirit.

> ***Jesus doesn't so much want us to walk in His footsteps,***
> ***as to surrender to His desire to step into our shoes.***
> ***He wants to do 'in us' the very thing***
> ***that religion has been trying to do in its own strength.***

It's a hard thing to get our heads around, but it's necessary that we do if we are to live as souls set free by the blood of Jesus.

Jesus further explained this way of living in John 5:19-20 *(NLT)*, "I tell you the truth, the Son can do nothing by Himself, He can only do what He sees His Father doing, because whatever the Father does, the Son also does. For the Father loves the Son and shows Him all that He does".

This can all sound a bit cryptic without an understanding of the ways of the Spirit. The flesh waits on specific directions and then legalistically follows them to the letter of the law. The spirit operates differently – it knows the Father's heart and lives spontaneously from the nature of God.

Our liberated soul is now able to follow this model of living.

The Father's life flowed through Jesus. Without it, he couldn't do anything, John 5:26 *(HCS)*, "For just as the Father has life in Himself, so He has granted the Son to have life in Himself". Jesus set aside His glory and lived as a man just like us – He had no more power than we do. All He had was a clear view of His Father; He only did what He saw His Father doing.

And now the Father's life flows through us. It starts with the Father, is granted to the Son, and then fills us up too. John 5:21, "For just as the Father raises the dead and gives them life, even so the Son gives life to whom He is pleased to give it".

Does He give it to us? Of course He does, it is why He came! John 10:10 *(ESV)* states, "I came that you might have life and have it abundantly". We have His life, but it won't flow in us until we *see and know* that we have it.

Jesus *saw* what His Father did, and in turn, we need to *see* with great clarity what Jesus did – then His life will flow through our souls.

> **We do not lack the divine life of the spirit;**
> **we only lack the ability to clearly see that we have it.**

Getting back to the first chapter of Ephesians, Paul declares the need for spiritual sight in verses 17-19, "I keep asking that the God of our Lord Jesus Christ, the glorious Father, may give you the spirit of wisdom and revelation, so that you may know Him better. I pray also that the eyes of your heart may be enlightened in order that you may know the hope to which He has called you, the riches of His glorious inheritance in the saints, and His incomparably great power for us who believe".

Paul doesn't pray that we would get anything new. He prays that we would see what we have got.

> **This is how the redeemed soul operates.**
> **It lives out of the truth that is apparent to the spirit.**

The body has physical eyes, and the spirit has spiritual eyes, and they see completely different realities. The soul lives from the reality that it sees most clearly, and Paul encourages the soul to take in the vista which is on display to the spirit, and live from this as its primary truth.

In effect, Paul is saying that the soul will be guided through life by the thing that it sees most clearly. Our physical sight and our spiritual sight have both volunteered to be our lifelong tour guide, and only we can decide who we will appoint to the role.

In that context, it's easy to see the problem as it related to Adam. He gave up his spiritual sight and appointed his physical sight in its place, and then he set about constructing his life from a completely different reality.

CHAPTER 25
The Adventure

So now that Jesus has restored us to our original design, and has re-opened our blind spiritual eyes, it is up to us to discover how to live by this new view of things, the view of who we have become as a result of the cross of Christ.

As we slowly begin to take in this spiritual vista, and gain a fresh view of the Kingdom of God, the Holy Spirit becomes our tour guide through the adventure of life. Our old tour guide (the flesh) is retired, and the Holy Spirit begins to lead us into a life we never dreamt possible.

We become a living example of the scripture – "The Spirit gives life, the flesh counts for nothing".

And the best part of all is that this wonderful life is what God wants for us too. The Holy Spirit is finally able to do the very thing He was sent for – to reveal the life of Jesus to us. John 15:26, "When the Counsellor comes, whom I will send to you from the Father, the Spirit of truth who goes out from the Father, He will testify about me".

Now lies before us the adventure we were made for, *and it goes like this...*

The Holy Spirit knows us better than we know ourselves. The Holy Spirit is fully informed of our make-up, and just like Jeremiah of old, "Before God formed us in the womb, He knew us". He knows the best way to lead us into the best version of ourselves. In fact, He is delighted with the raw material He finds in us, and longs to show us how to live magnificently in a way that is completely true to our unique blend of character traits.

He doesn't have to remake us, the blood of Jesus did that, He simply wants to lead us into the best life possible now that we have been made perfect by Jesus.

The only thing He requires is that we boldly accept that the blood of Jesus has done its work in us. We cannot doubt the efficacy of the blood of Jesus because God has no plan B, nor is He holding anything back, we must conduct a thorough examination of the claims the bible makes about Jesus and our reborn condition, and decide, once and for all, if we will stake our life on it.

The Holy Spirit cannot lead us anywhere until we cross that line.

The Holy Spirit cannot lead the soul that is still committed to the thinking of Adam. We must leave it behind and begin to trust that Christ has finished the task He came for. Only then can the adventure begin.

The Holy Spirit's role is to testify about Jesus, He has no interest in attesting to the legacy of Adam. He cannot build upon Adam's legacy, He can only build upon the rock; Jesus.

Do you see what I am saying? The Holy Spirit has nothing to work with if we doubt that Jesus sacrifice was sufficient to present us holy before His Father. Similarly, He has nothing to work with if we continue to promote the efforts of the flesh for that purpose.

Yet if we believe that Jesus has perfected us, we are ready.

This is the way that Adam first lived. He dined upon the Tree of Life, and that diet of God's love and life enabled him to be led by the Spirit.

The idea of being 'led by the Spirit' is not only a New Testament concept, it began all the way back in the Garden of Eden when Adam first opened his eyes and was enveloped in the love of God.

As a tour guide the Holy Spirit is very experienced. He knows just how to blend the beautiful union we have with God and the remarkably unique soul that God gave us, and show us a life that suits us best.

He did it at first with Adam – it was creative, it was exhilarating and it released the very best of Adam. Adam was created in God's image, which means that he was creative too. God didn't restrict Adam's influence, quite the contrary, God gave Adam dominion over every living thing – and so Adam named every living creature. He didn't simply give them a word as a name, (cat, dog, cow), he defined the nature of their existence – much like God defined Paul's existence when he changed his name from Saul, God gave him a new identity.

And Jesus has given us a new name too,
He has re-defined our existence as the objects of God's love.

So, now we can see that being 'led by the Spirit' does not restrict us at all – it releases us. It does not constrain us into a small life, but liberates us into the biggest life possible.

The legacy of Adam's fallen thinking has convinced us that God is trying to keep the lid on us, that He doesn't value our unique characteristics, and would prefer that we be held within the neat boundaries of religion and lifestyle. It is convinced that God wants 'sameness', not diversity. That He wants people to conform to the mould, rather than be released to be their special self.

God values who we are; be it intellectual, creative, sporting, ambitious, artistic, mechanical… *whatever*. God put it all in there when He formed us in our mother's womb, and He is pleased with it. So it stands to reason that 'God's Spirit in us' will enable the best possible expression of who we are.

It's a bit like the difference between a brass band and a jazz band, they might both play the same song, but the jazz band provides for individual expression. The brass band (religion) has very set pieces for each musician to play, no one can step outside of the notes they are assigned. Whereas the jazz band (the Spirit), encourages individual expression. Each person interpreting the beauty of God's song in their own way – harmonizing and improvising around the melody of God's love as it wells up from their heart.

CHAPTER 26

My Genius

Imagine being a bystander during the time of creation. It was an explosion of all of the creative impulses of God, yet it was perfection, the results speaking for themselves – the creative nature of God at work.

The Holy Spirit as our tour guide is in possession of the same creative nature. He sees possibilities we have not even contemplated, and He knows how to connect the vibrant life of the Spirit with the genius of our soul.

The expression of this 'genius' is only hampered by one thing – our inbuilt desire to be the 'life-source' as well. But as we lean back into Christ as the source of our being, the true magnificence of the soul finds fulfilment and expression. It's the way God designed us to be.

Jesus gave us a beautiful picture of this in John 15, where he uses the illustration of the vine and the branches; "No branch can bear fruit by itself; it must remain in the vine. Neither can you bear fruit unless you remain in me".

The diversity of fruitfulness is the soul's genius – fruit which is pleasing to the eye, tasty, nourishing, and full of life. We are the branches that bear the fruit and Jesus is the vine. He provides the life that gives the branch its fruitful expression. Without the vine, the fruit withers and dies.

> *Walking in the Spirit is all about 'remaining in Christ',*
> *that is our only part to play.*

Fruitfulness is the result, a fruitfulness from the life of Christ rather than one that is manmade.

We, as the human race, have lived for so long without Spirit-energized fruitfulness that we don't quite know how it works. And we don't know how to embrace our original design for fear that it might not work. We have lost the knack of drawing life from the vine, and doubt that such a Spirit-energized life is actually possible. This is what the Holy Spirit desires to re-awaken within us.

To a large extent, this dilemma is the result of the way the human soul has operated since Adam took leave of God's presence. We have inserted formulas, processes, and systems in place of the person of Jesus.

The unregenerate soul thrives on systems and formulas. It wants to know what to do to engage God into our lives.

But there is no 'list of steps' or 'tried and true methods', and Christian self-help books, or 'how to' manuals (no matter how well conceived), still leave us attempting to climb our way up to God. In that regard, our unregenerate soul has attempted to create God in its own image. It wants God to respond to the methodology of religion. Yet, He only responds to our faith in the blood of Jesus.

So the first thing the Holy Spirit does as we embark on our new Spirit walk is to shine the spotlight back onto Jesus. He cannot do anything for us until we stop trying to impress Him with our religious aerobics, and fix our eyes on Jesus, the author and perfector of our faith.

And as we let go of our earth-made securities, we start being carried aloft by the breath of God. This new life is like the flight of a bird, because it is so light in its touch and so free in its movement. The scripture found in John 3:8 comes to mind, "The wind blows wherever it pleases. You hear its sound, but you cannot tell where it comes from or where it is going. So it is with everyone born of the Spirit".

The touch of the Spirit upon us seems so light that we hardly know we are being directed at all. Such is the intimacy that we share. We are indeed one, yet my soul is free to respond to His light touch in its own way. The Holy Spirit seems to enjoy the freedom of my soul as much as I do.

*There is no constraint or coercion
because God's Spirit within me has the same deep desire that I do
- that I would live spontaneously free,
yet totally surrendered to His all-encompassing love.*

Just like Adam in that first moment when he saw God, I am filled. Filled in a way that is hard to explain because there is no weight in this filling, no burden attached to it, just the joy of being carried on the wings of God.

With effortless energy, His love carries me into new realms. And in each realm He is there with more life, more love, and more of His in-dwelling presence. I feel like I am living in heaven and on earth both at the same time.

And I begin to be me.

CHAPTER 27

The Light

The 'me' that was locked up inside Adam's foolish scheme has been freed to walk out into the light of day and what a light it is! John wrote, "In Him was life, and that life was the light of men". I have been set free to walk in the light, and I am beginning to glimpse the glory of it all.

It's tentative at first. Being trapped for so long gets inside you; we don't instinctively know how to be free. But the Holy Spirit is patient, leading us one step at a time into the blazing glory of God's unconditional love.

So we begin in a kind of squinting way, unaccustomed to the light of God, unfamiliar with walking in its brightness – lacking confidence that we should even be doing it in the first place.

But the Holy Spirit won't have it, He knows our design and He knows the heart of God. He is determined that we would live in the light, even as He is in the light – *He will see us through.* When Adam remade humanity, he made us to be shadow-dwellers, more familiar with the vagaries of man-generated goodness, and uncertain and tentative about living in the brilliance of God's holiness. But our Holy Spirit guide knows the way back to our real self, and He won't rest until we are safely home and engulfed in the glory of God.

It's funny to think that someone else knows me better than I know myself. It's as if all the years and centuries of human history mean very little to the Holy Spirit – He doesn't see me in them. He sees me in Jesus. History has been erased; its hold on me no longer exists as far as God is concerned. The only thing that exists is the fact that God made me to be the perfect object of His love, and Jesus unlocked the prison of my past.

There is an eagerness about it all, as if the Holy Spirit has stepped over all the human reasons why I should delay and said, "Enough, your inheritance awaits, do not keep the King of Glory waiting. His heart is bursting with desire that you would be the person He made you."

> **What did you say?**
> **God is waiting for me to let Him love me?**

And it dawns on me at last; I am squinting into the true God, not the one that Adam made in his own image. The gate to my heart has been closed for too long by Adam's determination to earn God's love. God hasn't been keeping me out – I have been keeping *Him* out!

My spirit already knows this. My spirit is exposed to this truth because it is the atmosphere of the presence of God. Everyone in heaven knows this. And now the blood of Christ has returned this truth to the souls of men dwelling on earth too.

Imagine, God's love is as real and unconditional for me as I walk out my days on earth, as it will be when I step over the threshold of heaven and see Him face to face. As far as God is concerned, I am walking in the full measure of His glory now, and His greatest desire for me is that I would see it and live the liberated life it offers.

Light! It is breaking through the shell of my man-made securities, cracking open my self-doubts, and showing me the truth that was there all along. I have been bathed in the brilliance of God's love the whole time! It's just that the mad experiment of Adam had pulled the shades down.

Come into it!

Come and live here!

Come back to your origins, those ancient days when you walked freely in the light of God because it was your nature to do so. It is your design that you can stand in the blazing glory of God and allow His love to search out every dark corner, every shame, every regret, and fill every shaded space with His astonishing grace and kindness.

> **God is back in – He has got me.**

I feel myself inexplicably drawn to His magnetic love. My reluctance is falling away, my doubts are dissolving and the gate of my heart is gently but firmly eased open by the Holy Spirit. He knows what I need, and I find myself running free as I have never run before – straight into the love embrace of the great lover of my soul.

I am possessed by a love that cannot be quenched.

And that possessing releases my soul to be the genius He made it.

We are all genius, God doesn't create inferior souls. Sure, some may rise to the lofty heights of human achievement, but that's not the genius I am talking about. It's not the genius that God contemplated in His making of us.

God's kind of genius is not especially related to human achievement, but rather to the ability of the soul of man to drink-in the wonder and goodness of the presence of God, and to live a great life from that resource. Human achievement has hidden something magnificent from our view; *that we are made to be carriers of the glory of God.*

It's in us all. God is indiscriminate; His genius is just as present in the dull and lowly as in the high and mighty. Sometimes the dull and lowly grasp it easier for the lack of self-made alternatives.

It is perhaps the hardest of all truths for the human soul to grasp, that the measure of our worth is not to be found in our earthly achievements, no matter how altruistic. We have a built in resistance to our God-given nature, always attempting to contain it within our self-generated goodness. But the true genius of our soul is only liberated when we cease from striving, and let God love us for *His* reasons.

This love remakes the 'me' that Adam broke.

God values His original creation of humankind so highly that He sent Jesus to die, so that now I can live in that original creation again in freedom and boldness. This is God's plan; it has always been His plan.

God changes not. His intentions for humanity are what they have always been – that we would be carried through life by His love.

Dare I also begin to love my design as God does? Dare I believe that I can be loved so much that my human weakness doesn't matter? And dare I think about myself in a way that reflects the opinion God has of me?

Being trapped is my past. Being free is my future. But how do I learn to live in freedom when captivity is all I have known? The Holy Spirit knows how to do it, because He can see the end. He knows the remarkable capacity of the blood of Christ to transform, and He sees me as transformed now, even though I am as yet barely out of captivity.

The light of Jesus does this. It allows a new image of 'me' to come into focus. It shows me the view God has of me, now that Jesus has done His work. The blind that Adam pulled down over the real 'me' is drawn up again by the power of Jesus' sacrifice – and my original genius is once again on view. Not so much on view for God, or the angels, or even for other people, but on view for me – God wants me to know who I am.

Walking in the light is all about seeing what God sees.

It's about understanding both God and myself from a new perspective – God's perspective. It is a perspective that is diametrically opposite to the perspective I received from Adam, because the blind of human achievement has been drawn up, and the glory of God can once again blaze into my soul.

We don't (by nature) have an accurate view of God, we see Him through the filter of human achievement, but when we remove that filter a completely different view of God is presented to us. You wouldn't think that something good, like human effort, could block out the true image of God, but it does. This is because the filter of human achievement has added something to God that is actually not there – conditions to be satisfied for living in His presence.

In John 17:24 we read, "Father, I want those you have given me to be with me where I am, and to *see my glory*, the glory you have given me because you loved me before the creation of the world", and also in verse 22, "I have given them *the glory that you gave me*, that they may be one as we are one".

This is the unfiltered way God sees us – 'Jesus is filled with the glory of God, and He has given that glory to us'. We are ablaze with the glory of God just like Jesus. The blood of Jesus has achieved something that human effort couldn't; it has re-made us to be carriers of the extraordinary glory of God.

The angels in heaven see this. In fact, the whole of creation is standing-by in eager anticipation of it. Romans 8:19 says, "For the creation waits in eager expectation for the children of God to be revealed". When will we finally let the light of God in, and see it too? *We have been remade just like Jesus.*

CHAPTER 28
The Glory

The implications of all that I am saying are really quite astounding (even shocking), so in order to lay hold of them, we need new eyes.

I am saying that there is a glory about us that we cannot see, and it is the same glory that Jesus had when He walked the earth. The thinking of Adam concealed it from our view, but Jesus had no such problem, He saw this glory as plain as day.

We do not need to do anything special to activate this stunning truth, all we need to do is open our eyes and see it, and live in it by faith. It is a glory that radiates from Christ in us, the invisible radiance of God shining out of our spirits.

Fallen humanity is unique in its *in*ability to see it, remember the demoniac in Mark 5:6-7, *(NAS)* "Seeing Jesus from a distance, he ran up and bowed down before Him; and shouting with a loud voice, he said, 'What business do we have with each other, Jesus, Son of the Most High God? I implore you by God, do not torment me!'". The ordinary people around Jesus couldn't see this glory; it took a being with spiritual sight to see it. Every spiritual being in heaven and hell can clearly see the glory of God that radiates from His presence in us, and we can see it too… *by faith.*

The entire mass of heavenly beings is stunned by the awesome presence of Jesus that radiates from every pore of our new nature. They are amazed that the work of the cross can have achieved so much in people who were so utterly depraved, *and they wonder when we will see it too.*

When we see it, everything changes. And it begins to leak out of us.

> ***This glorious light is uncontainable,***
> ***that's how the glory of God works***
> ***– the only way it won't shine out is by unbelief.***

When we see the work that Christ completed on the cross, and hide ourselves in its truth, a wonderful thing happens – we become the instruments of that truth. We become the instruments that play and improvise around the melody of God's love. He is the song, the life of the song is in Him, and we have the glorious joy of being the instruments that play Him.

The magnificence of His song fills us to overflowing and the glorious tune of His love wells up and pours forth from our souls – each person playing in the great orchestra, contributing their own unique outpouring in the symphony of His love.

This is what we were made for.

His Spirit fills us, His breath gives our notes their being, and the heart of God is heard throughout all the world. Those who hear it may not even perceive it, they may not consciously grasp that God has sung His love to them. They may have only perceived a friend's touch, a stranger's smile, a kind word said in passing, but the song has registered in their spirits – God is drawing them back.

As we fix our eyes on Jesus, the author and perfector of our faith (the great conductor of the orchestra of God's love), the song springs up from within us. We hardly know it is happening because there is no human effort required (but that we gaze upon the love of God).

This is the great commission – go in to all the world and sing my love song. You can because I am going back to my Father and He will fill you with a new song. Psalm 40:3 anticipated this moment, "He put a new song in my mouth, a hymn of praise to our God. Many will see and fear the Lord and put their trust in Him".

People will see God and put their trust in Him as He plays His song of love through us.

We are not, *by nature,* aware that this expression of the love of God for humanity flows from us automatically as we confidently rest in the cross of Christ. Our natural inclination is to think that it is the result of a deliberate effort on our part to represent or emulate Christ. Not so, the only thing we bring to the table is confidence in Christ, and then His life 'in us' does the work.

Jesus *(the last Adam)* was the first human being *(since Adam fell)*, to naturally rest in this automatic flow of spiritual life, and He has given us the privilege to share in this 'rest'. *When we hide ourselves in His ability, our ability is sidelined.*

It might sound bold, even presumptuous, to apply the realities of Christ's time on earth to ourselves. The fallen nature of humanity shrinks back from such boldness, preferring humility and unworthiness, but Christ went to the cross that we might be carriers of the glory of God, it behoves us to shrink back from His legacy.

> **It becomes right and proper for us to carry the glory of God in earthen vessels because God has made it right, rather than our human striving making it right.**

This 'glory of God' that we carry around in our earthly vessels is the result of that mysterious union which the flesh kept hidden through the ages – 'Christ in me, *the hope of glory*', Colossians 1:27. The hope of glory becomes the reality of our lives as we lose ourselves in the certainty of His work in us. 'Christ in me' does it all.

I don't mean to portray this activity of the Spirit as spooky or unnerving. It is, in fact, a very natural instinct for someone who has looked Christ in the eye and declared 'from this moment forward, you are the source of my being'. Dining daily on 'the Tree of Life' as the source of our existence is the way God made us to live.

It's not the same as participating in religious or spiritual activities (though these may still be present in our lives); rather, it is putting all of our confidence in the spiritual activities of Christ to carry us through.

In John 6:28-29 they asked Jesus, "What must we do to do the works that God requires?" Jesus answered "The work of God is this: to believe in the one He has sent". There is just one thing we need to do for the work that God wants to take place – believe in Jesus!

This belief *(which is much more than mere mental accent),* has an outworking in the realm of the spirit which is invisible in the natural realm. The glorious light of God fills us. It's not a visible light, but a light which is invisible to the natural eye, yet this glorious light radiates throughout eternity.

You could say that we are plugged into Christ – He is the power source and we are the light bulb.

It took me a long time to grasp this truth. I spent about 55 years doing all the things that Christians do – participating in all the programs, applying all the biblical principles, exercising passion and zeal, and finally, after life had worn me down, I came to the end of myself and stopped trying. It was only then that I began to understand that I don't generate the light by my religious lifestyle; I am simply a human vessel through whom the light that Christ has generated shines.

Sure, I generated a dim glow through my religious fervour and commitment, but it was nothing compared to the blazing glory of Christ. In the end, my dim glow was irrelevant in the presence of His blazing light.

I mentioned back at the start of this book that we are a tripartite being – body, soul and spirit. Our spirit is the real 'us'. It is our spirit which radiates the glory of God. Our spirit gets this glory directly from its union with Christ. So it's important that we consider ourselves to be primarily spiritual people, it all begins in the realm of the spirit. And then, once our soul catches on, it lives out on the earth the truth which is the normal environment of our spirit.

If we look for the visible (physical) evidence first, then we are not believing in the truth. This results in the physical realm taking precedence over the spiritual realm (our true home).

So, when Jesus says "I have given them the glory which you gave to me", we must elevate that truth to be the absolute fact of our lives by determining once and for all that the cross of Christ has completed its transformative work in us. Then, ultimately, in its own time, the physical realm will fall into line with the spiritual reality.

The outcome of such a way of thinking is that we begin to see ourselves differently. When we walk into a room, we perceive the glory of God entering with us, radiating and touching every person and need in that room. In every conversation, the Spirit of Jesus is present, touching, healing and restoring, as we rest in His unconditional love.

> *We do not 'work up' or 'press in' for this presence –*
> *we simply see that it is the outcome of the cross of Christ,*
> *and live in it by faith.*

2 Corinthians 3:18 *(BSB)* puts it beautifully; "And we, who with unveiled faces all reflect the glory of the Lord, are being transformed into His image with intensifying glory, which comes from the Lord, who is the Spirit".

The 'unveiling' of our faces is the removing of the thinking of Adam, and the 'transformation into His image with intensifying glory' comes from God's Spirit, not us. The intensification of His glory takes place as we remove the veil of human effort that separates us from God, and stand before Him, naked of self-made worth. Then, we spontaneously reflect *His* glory.

There is another beautiful scripture like this one in 1 John 3:2 *(NLT)*, "Dear friends, we are already God's children, but He has not yet shown us what we will be like when Christ appears. But we do know that we will be like Him, for we will see Him as He really is".

We become 'like Christ' when we see Him as He is. For the majority of Christians, this will take place after they die and meet Him in heaven, but for a few, they will see Him as He is now. They will lift the veil of Adam's thinking, and the intense glory of Jesus will overtake them, even though they still remain on earth.

Jesus didn't have to try hard to walk in the intense glory of His Father, nor did He need to drum it up with overt spiritual activities. He simply saw His Father's love for Him, and that unveiled exposure to His Father's glory caused it to be reflected through Him.

In other words, the intense glory of God, which accompanied Jesus through his life, was the bi-product of the fact that Jesus rested in His Father's unconditional love.

The same is true of us.

Only for us, we see the Father's unconditional love expressed through the sacrifice of Jesus, and we rest in it as the great truth of our lives.

It is an amazing thing to think that the glory of God resides in us just by believing. It seems too spectacular an outcome to be obtained with so little effort, yet, that is the way of the Spirit. Everything we possess of spiritual worth is received by faith alone.

So, perhaps we should come to terms with the astonishing nature of faith, instead of being distracted by the flesh's insistence of having a role to play.

CHAPTER 29
A New Identity

If we can push to one side the clamouring of the flesh for its share of the spotlight, and come to terms with the staggering potential within each of us to live by faith, then a whole new way of living opens up to us.

The flesh is determined to convince us that faith is a direct result of human effort – that it is a combination of tenacity, zealousness and commitment, which we apply to a stubborn object to get it to yield. A 'never say die' application of spiritual principles and actions that result in the demolition of the problem we are facing. Such activities as loud prayer and bold demonstrations of spiritual aggression come to mind, as though the greater the human effort, the greater the spiritual power.

But nothing could be further from the truth. Faith is more about what we see than what we do. It is the outcome of standing at the foot of the cross, gazing at the claims it makes and asking Jesus what it was all about, and slowly it dawns on us that Jesus completed the impossible – He made me as good as God, and faith springs up from that revelation.

And without that revelation, faith is merely the pumped up efforts of religious zeal.

Faith is seeing something that does not yet exist in the physical realm. Human activity is of no use here, only the activity of the cross can create something we can see from something which is invisible.

There is an invisible connection linking all of the outcomes of the cross of Christ. They may seem to be unrelated and have separate benefits, but, in fact, each one is just a different facet of the one over-arching thing that Jesus accomplished.

Jesus dealt with our sin. He crucified our old nature and rebirthed us with His own. He gave us access to God's presence, and filled us with His glory.

He brought our spirit into perfect divine union with Himself and His Father. He gave us the Holy Spirit as our true spiritual self. He restored our soul to its original design. And He invited us to be the instruments that play His love song. All of these things are not separate, unrelated outcomes; they are all part of the same package deal, which He accomplished on the cross.

We tend to think of the outcomes of the cross of Christ as being separately obtained, that each one comes to us as we progressively lay hold of it, and that God distributes these outcomes to us as we grow and mature in our Christian walk.

In reality these outcomes all became ours in the very same instant in time. One instant we had nothing, the next instant we have everything. The reason is that these outcomes are all contained within the one ever-arching fact of our salvation – <u>we have been made new</u>.

We are not what we once were.

God has nothing more to give us – we have the whole package and all that remains is that we see who we have become, and live in our new identity.

The only thing that separates us from living on the earth just like Jesus did is that we can't see that such a way of living is available to us. Jesus was no different to us, the bible is very clear that He set aside His Godly status and became a man just like us – but He was able to see something which the legacy of Adam had obscured from us, we have all that we need for life and godliness – 2 Peter 1:3.

I don't believe Jesus accomplished the complete restoration of our identity, and then left it hidden from us so that it is of no benefit until we die and go to heaven. To me, that would seem like He didn't complete the task He came for. I believe it is possible for every believer to walk as Jesus walked, and that the ability to see who we are is within each of us.

What a shame to live our whole lives as just a fraction of the new person that Christ recreated us to be, all for the lack of spiritual sight.

So it begs the question; 'how do we get the eyes of our hearts working?', 'How do we awaken the sight that Paul prayed about in Ephesians 1:18, "I pray also that the eyes of your heart may be enlightened"?' I don't believe that someone with Paul's insight would pray such a prayer if it was not possible for ordinary garden variety Christians like us to obtain the outcome of it.

So many of us have been stuck in a cycle of not receiving very much from God at all, we have gotten so used to meagre hand-outs that our expectation is at rock bottom – *Adam's legacy is doing its thing to Christians all over the world.*

The future doesn't have to be that way.

The prayer that Paul prayed for the Ephesian church (and all of us that followed, is now a reality). We can see again.

This sight can be activated or shut-down according to our understanding of the work that Christ accomplished. Faith cannot spring to life if it is in opposition to our understanding of who we are as a result of Christ's sacrifice. It cannot be wrung out of us like water from a sponge – it overflows like rivers of living water from the life of Christ welling up from within us.

In short, if we are to actually live out His life in us, we must see with clarity that Christ has made us worthy to walk in His Spirit. If we can't see our worthiness, then our faith will remain stuck in the unbelief of Adam. And God will not oppose our faith (be it positive or negative); because it is the currency of heaven.

We Christians have become so adept at asking God to do things in opposition to our faith, we think that by pleading, or begging, God will relent and His resistance will crumble because of our many and desperate words. That's simply not the way of it. If it came down to relenting, rest assured, God relented when He sent Christ to die. God relented long ago, now it's up to us to perceive our true nature and walk in it, as He created us to do.

Adam made a mess of faith. It used to work so easily before he decided humanity could do better without it. He came up with his own overt alternative (religion) – doing the 'right thing' to impress a God who didn't need impressing. And so, the God kind of faith drifted into a distant memory.

We have a better recollection of Adam's way, than God's way. But the Holy Spirit remembers, and He won't rest until He blows the cobwebs out of our souls and shows us the work of Christ over and over and over again, *until we get it.*

The Holy Spirit does not want us to believe a fairy tale, or put our lives in the hands of a theory. Nor is He showing us a far stretch of the real truth. He is not at all reckless in His ambitions for us; He is showing us the absolute facts of our existence – a truth that will transform us if we let it, a truth that cost Jesus His life so that we might live free.

It is a truth that is as close as our next breath, just waiting for us to discover it, waiting for us to get to the end of ourselves and lean-in to God's love, *just because we can.*

The only thing that can thwart the Holy Spirits agenda is 'us' – our guilt, our doubt, our pride.

It doesn't matter to God how bad we've been. He doesn't care what we think about our past lives, He just wants us to trust Him with everything, so that He can turn our messed up lives into His beautiful music. He can do it now – we don't need to wait until we have our lives sorted out. He simply longs to hear us say, 'I'm coming home to you'.

He longs for us with a love as big as the universe. He made it big so we know His love is big. He made a universe that is expanding at an unbelievable rate, so that we could believe that His love knows no bounds.

> *If we could just see the scale and nature of His love –*
> *we would let go of all our inhibitions in a heartbeat.*
> *We would entrust every fibre of our existence into His care,*
> *casting all caution to the wind.*

The Holy Spirit is determined for us to know.

And we are beginning to know. The light of God is peeping in through the edges of Adam's blind. The unrestrained love and life of God is breaking into the darkest of places in the world. The souls of humankind are again glimpsing the truth Adam knew at the beginning – that God loves us because of who He is, not because of who we are.

The fact of the matter is that all of this truth is ours right now. God is not still working on it or preparing it for us – we are in it, and He has got us.

> *A smile begins to form, 'Yes, it is true isn't it?*
> *Even for me. Today is my day to agree with God.'*

The fight has gone out of me, all resistance is gone. He wanted me, and now He has got me, warts and all.

I am His; in Him and through Him, filled by Him and for Him. No more waiting, I am home.

The light I find myself in is very different to the light that shines on the earth. This light is generated by God Himself. The purpose of the light on the earth is so that we can see where we are going, and what we are doing, by illuminating our physical world. It is generated by natural means, for a natural purpose. The light of God produces the same result in me in the spiritual realm. It exposes me to the truth – God is love, God is good, God is with us. My spirit instinctively knows what to do as it is exposed to God's light – God's light is spiritual and it produces a spiritual outcome in me.

The spiritual outcome produced in me by the light of God is that I become secure in His love.

God's light has a washing or purifying effect, 1 John 1:7, "But if we walk in the light, as He is in the light, we have fellowship with one another, and the blood of Jesus His Son cleanses us from all sin". My new cleansed condition gives me a sense of security that religion couldn't. It does in an instant what religion attempted to do over a lifetime.

This security brings out the best in me, I am released to live a spontaneously great life because I am free to be the real me. God is pleased – He always wanted me to be me. He imagined me that way before I was formed in my mother's womb.

God's plan and purpose for me is wrapped up in this one thing – that I become secure in His love.

CHAPTER 30

Clean

Being in the presence of God is quite unlike being in the presence of a human being. The love, life and goodness that emanates continually from His being washes over and through us, and we become like Him. No other being has that characteristic, the ability to cleanse someone simply by being in their presence.

The continually cleansing light of God is the thing that Adam stepped out of, and so he destined all of humanity to a self-cleansing life – and the whole human race has been exhausted, trying to clean up ourselves ever since.

Imagine the scene where Jesus washes the disciple's feet. He is giving them an example of how to serve each other. Jesus declares to them, "unless I wash you, you have no part in me". Impetuous Peter wants to take it a step further and have his hands and head washed too, but Jesus clarifies to Peter that *'he is already clean'*.

This was Adam's problem – he wanted to wash himself.

But Jesus made it clear that only *He* does the real washing. His presence cleanses us – that's why Peter was already clean.

And now as we serve others, He washes them too. My only task is to let him wash me by remaining in His love. My tour guide the Holy Spirit has led me to this place, I am sitting with Jesus and He is declaring that I am clean, just like He did with Peter.

The security of being clean is remarkably empowering. The light of God, which is my new nature, goes with me into every circumstance. I can feel fear falling away and faith is rising – just by being in His cleansing light. Now that I know I am clean, my doubts about God's presence in and with me are falling away too. I am becoming more confident to be me as I grasp the truth that He is happy with me just as I am.

Not pumped up with my best, but resting in His best.

There is so much to speak of when contemplating our spiritual existence. The glory of God (though unseen by the natural eye), is the atmosphere we live in. We cannot escape from its penetrating radiance. *Not that we would want to.*

It holds us in God's perfection, always filling us with His holiness – *even when we slip up in the natural realm.* We cannot undo or even limit the endless flow of righteousness from God's heart to ours, "even if our hearts condemn us, – because God is greater than our hearts, and He knows everything", 1 John 3:20.

What an amazing statement "God is greater than our hearts". His transforming flow of life and love will not be interrupted by our sense of unworthiness or guilt.

It seems to me that humanity is stuck in the thinking that God is not greater than our hearts. That our heart's tendency toward self-condemnation is stronger than God's ability to fill us with His light. And that God must stand by helpless, unable to love us until we make ourselves good enough.

It seems to me that we think Adam was stronger than Jesus, and that we are stuck in a cycle that won't end until we die – a cycle of trying to be good enough, or to clean ourselves up… but never quite measuring up.

It seems to me that the whole human race doesn't know what to do with Jesus. We know what to do with Adam because we instinctively 'get him', but as much as we try, we don't really know how to fit Jesus into the scheme of things. So we join His club and sing His songs, without actually knowing how to simply be in His cleansing light.

That's why God needs to be greater than our hearts. Because, when we are left to our own devices, our hearts condemn us as unworthy of God. Our hearts are, by nature, better at reflecting the realities of the natural realm, than the higher reality of the spiritual realm.

The spiritual realm knows better. It won't have any of Adams self-generated righteousness – we are worthy because Jesus has given us His worth. *End of story!*

So, the fact is, we are in the cleansing light whether we like it or not.

There is no Christian on the earth who is not radically bathed in the glorious, righteousness-giving light of the Most High God. It is the over-arching fact of our lives. We are in the Kingdom of God, and the atmosphere of that kingdom is God's radiant goodness. And this makes everything that is exposed to it clean and good.

If we don't *feel* clean, then that is our problem not God's – He has done all He can do.

CHAPTER 31

In the Light

Now that we are in that light, and the light of God has 'got us', we are offered a most extraordinary opportunity by the Holy Spirit – we can also walk in the light.

The light of God is not content to simply resolve our sin problem – it can also empower us to live in a way we never dreamed possible. The bible calls it 'walking in the Spirit'.

It is like living in another country – the difference between living in North Korea and Australia; dictatorship v. democracy. Most of the citizens of North Korea know of no other way to live, it is the only way they have ever known or heard of. As far as they are concerned, this is how the whole world lives.

But, imagine their surprise and delight to learn that there is another way. A way that is free of oppression and control, a way that allows them to live true to their potential, and to flourish as the unique person they are.

Such is the difference between walking in the ways of Adam, and walking in the Spirit.

The ways of Adam have hidden this alternative way of living from view for so long that much of Christianity doesn't even realise that such an option is available to them. We have settled for a form of Christianity which acknowledges the work of Christ, but doesn't actually know how to live in it.

And worse than that, we have constructed our own form of freedom as a poor copy of the true release given to us by Christ. It is a freedom that is still imprisoned in the thinking of Adam – so it is actually no freedom at all.

It's no better than being a commander in the North Korean army. He has authority over others, but he himself is also controlled, so he remains trapped in a dictatorship which has the potential to execute him should he ever slip-up. It would be better to get out of that country all together. Even though there is the appearance of safety, it would be better to escape to true freedom across the border.

We know that we would never deliberately choose to live in North Korea after having the opportunity to live in Australia, yet, that is the scam that satan has pulled on humanity. We have opted to live under the dictatorship of Adam's thinking when our real home is available to us, ready and waiting for our occupation and enjoyment.

In Galatians 5:1 we read, "It is for freedom that Christ has set us free. Stand firm, then, and do not let yourselves be burdened again by a yoke of slavery". This slavery is not a life of rampant sin, it is a life controlled by the imprisoned thinking of Adam.

This scripture is telling us this: Just because we have been set free by the blood of Christ doesn't mean we are automatically going to live as a free person – for that, we need to abandon the thinking of a slave, and begin to think like a son. Jesus has set us free, but He cannot force us to live free. He has swung the prison door wide open, and invited us to walk out into the light. Whether we do or not is up to us.

Religion is a prison.

Don't confuse religion with church involvement, they are not the same. Religion is the practicing of a list of activities and observances to satisfy God, and attract His favour, blessing, and love. But God is already satisfied with us because we have received the righteousness of Christ. Religion attempts to add something to the sacrifice of Jesus that God does not require to qualify us – *lifestyle and religious practices.*

Even good practices like prayer, bible reading and worship are an affront to God if done to attract His favour, which is already freely given by the blood of Jesus.

The prison of religion cannot accept that there is another way to live. Neither can it accept that this other way is actually God's way – it can only perceive self-based Christianity.

The prison of religion is like North Korea, it obscures from our view the option of freedom.

The prison of religion knows that it cannot keep us from being set free by the light – it just doesn't want us to *live in* that freedom. The work of Christ has accomplished the task it was sent for; we have been remade back into our original self. The broken version of humanity has been reborn anew, but religion is determined to keep us living in the derelict of the past.

There is security in the old derelict if it is all we have ever known. Some prisoners re-offend after their release, just to be back where they feel most at home. And we, too, have an affinity for the ways of religion – it fits us like an old pair of shoes, and we don't like the notion of breaking in a new pair.

The ways of the Spirit are a new adventure – a brave new world that beckons us. The Spirit calls us out of religion to fly upon the winds of God. We don't know where they might blow, but we know they will be gentle and fair because that is the nature of God.

Adam's religion holds us in its familiarity – we know how it works. But the Spirit calls us to abandon ourselves to the freedom of the life of Christ.

Take your pick!

CHAPTER 32
God's Plan

Perhaps the thing we have most taken to be true from Adam's legacy is that God has a pattern worked out for us – a divine blueprint for our lives which is a blend of His will and purposes, the great commission, and generally using the ups and downs of life to get us into the shape He wants.

Like a play that is written from the end back to the start, God has an ultimate outcome in mind and so He arranges a myriad of events, circumstances and divine appointments all neatly ordered to get us to the end point He has mapped out for us. And that this small piece of the jigsaw fits into a much bigger picture, which is the combination of all the lives of His children. He takes His master plan and neatly weaves in our prayers and requests, being careful to balance the needs of all against the wishes of the individual. He manoeuvres our conflicts, sicknesses, heart aches and troubles, and works it all into a tapestry of divine proportions.

The best hope for us is to somehow influence God to err in our favour, and produce a lifetime of relatively pleasing events and outcomes.

I don't buy it.

Nor do I buy the notion that our relationship with God is dependent on the application of some human initiative, that we Christians touch God when we utter our prayers and when we go about our religious observances, but He is rendered helpless until we do. Is our relationship with God really dependent on the satisfactory performance of our rituals? And is God in the grip of inertia until we present our act of homage to Him… *or is there something much higher at play?*

Adam handed down a way of perceiving God's involvement in our lives which is skewed at best, and more likely just plain wrong. It is as if he made a conclusion about God, and wrote it into the family legend. It has been accepted without question for so long now that we daren't examine it for fear that the whole thing might unravel.

That; just like we don't know what to do to get God's help, God doesn't know what to do with us – until we somehow impose ourselves on His benevolence.

So he waits patiently for us to present our petitions and religious observances, weighs them in the balance, and responds with the best He can do under the circumstances. And if we are lucky, and we catch Him on a good day and all the planets line up – we might get what we ask for. And perhaps, if we labour the point, and impose on God's goodness with extended expressions of our need and His mercy, we might touch His tolerant affection and our wishes be granted.

But, is the King of Kings, the creator of everything visible and invisible, really sitting at His great big writing desk in the sky, waiting for us to bring our pieces of paper to Him, so that He can put them all in order and then start the complex process of changing history to meet our needs? – *Especially when two earnest Christians ask for opposite things.*

Forgive my ramblings...

Not that God couldn't process the affairs of humanity that way if He chose, but have we boxed God into a human-like mode of operation that makes more sense in our heads than His? Quite frankly, I find the notion of complex plans and purposes far too convoluted for a God who created the whole thing in six days. It's all a bit too eleventh hour for me, waiting and hoping that God will 'kick in to action', while we bravely keep our optimism up in the face of life's troubles. *I mean; do we really think God is impotent until we lay out our petitions before Him?* **And more than that, why does He always wait till the last minute to answer our prayers?**

This whole question of God's involvement in our lives really is becoming one of those things that has the potential to unravel the status quo...

This life that we lead in Adam's footsteps asks so much of us that at times, that all we can do is dump the lot at God's feet. We really want Him to have a plan, because if He doesn't, how are we going to explain the mess we so often find ourselves in? How else can we make sense of it all? There must be some greater point to it all that might bring hope, and shed light on all the randomness.

Surely the kind of God who could put the whole of creation together in six days should also be able to put together a more robust process for involving Him in our lives than the satisfactory earthly performance of our assigned religious rituals – even good rituals like, quiet times, prayer and bible study.

Stay with me now, this is heading somewhere...

CHAPTER 33
Dominion

'God is in control' *someone said;* and far be it from me to unravel something that we have all pinned our lives on. He is God, after all. He created everything so He must be in control – and if He isn't who is?

At last we arrive at the crux of the matter… 'Who is in control?'

We have no doubt that God *could* be in control… if that was the way He had planned it. But does that mean He is in control? We have no doubt that He *can* act sovereignly if He so chose, but is that what He has chosen?

So we approach God tentatively, almost superstitiously, not quite game to live by faith, and not quite ready to let Him go. We don't call it superstition (we have much more sophisticated names for it), but all we actually seem to be doing is little more than trying to manipulate God with our best religious practices, and spiritual principles, hoping that we are in sync with the broader Christian community… *and hoping that they know what's going on more than we do.*

We adopt the methodology of the herd because it's all we know.

But, what if we are all flying blind, hoping that the navigation instruments handed down to us by Adam are sufficient to guide us home, yet second guessing ourselves because of a nagging thought that everyone has missed something very important… *and we are not quite sure what it is.*

A crazy thought pops in to my head.

**Perhaps God handed control to us, and we didn't notice it.
He saw the magnificent accomplishments of the blood of Jesus,
and concluded that we were fully equipped to handle life.**

Not that God relinquished control through lack of interest or care, but that He did something even better than holding on to control, He gave us dominion as a gift. He gave us the 'right of rule' over the whole place, and said; 'it's yours now, enjoy', just like He did with Adam all those years ago. Adam did badly, he took that control and turned the whole thing on its head, but Jesus has given us back what Adam broke. He turned the whole thing right way up again, and gave us His Spirit to show us what to do with it.

Now, that would be a total reversal of Adam's way – God giving back to us what He initially gave to Adam… *dominion.* But what exactly is dominion, and how does it work?

I'm not suggesting that God is not intimately involved in our lives; I'm suggesting that God is actually more involved than most people think – *just differently.*

If all God does is get involved with us when we pray and ask for help, or when we gather together on Sundays and midweek fellowship meetings, then He is not really very involved at all – more of a sporadic involvement in proportion to our prayers and religious activities.

But imagine if you were in prayer one day and you asked God to be with you, and He spoke to you and said, 'If you like, I can be with you for every second of every day for the rest of your life – and you don't ever have to ask that question again'. Well, that is what He has actually said in Hebrews 13:5, "Never will I leave you; never will I forsake you."

God is already involved.

So involved, that He has done more than answer our cries for help and respond to our religious lifestyle – He has permanently moved in and brought with Him all of the benefits of the cross. He has laid out a banquet before us and invited us to help ourselves to His bounty whenever we like.

He has explained to us that we don't get in touch with Him when we pray. He has been completely in touch with us from the moment we first saw His love and asked Him to come into our hearts and lives.

We are joined at the hip!

Dominion is knowing that 'God in us' is our permanent identity, and then living freely and boldly from that reality. It is not trying to get God engaged into the issues of life, but confronting them with confidence and faith because He is already engaged by His presence in us.

If God is in us, then I find it quite confounding that we pray to Him as though He isn't.

You see, prayer is a different business now; it is based on the certainty that God is already engaged in the issues – the same as we are. Prayer is now a partnership; the power of the cross of Christ and my assurance in its effectiveness.

What a wonderful thing it is to talk to God about the concerns of life, and to rest in His love expressed on the cross. We know that He sent Jesus to die for us 'while we were yet sinners', so it stands to reason that He is just as mindful of each and every human need 'while we are in them'. He didn't need us to pray for our salvation before He saved us, and He doesn't *need* us to pray for Him to express His love to us now. Rather, prayer is now a daily partaking of heaven's bounty which has already been released to us at the cross.

> **Prayer is different now that He is in us,**
> **the immediacy of His presence changes everything.**

The fact is; He has gathered us into His kingdom where all things are in abundance, and given us the privilege of taking hold of the things of His kingdom as we need them, by faith.

God doesn't have two different ways of responding to our needs that He employs dependant on whether we come to Him with faith or prayer. It is *all* by faith, and prayer must be the expression of our assurance.

Much of modern Christianity has taken the Old Covenant element of human effort and overlaid it onto the New Covenant exhortation to pray, with the result that we attempt to move God by our persistence and determination, rather than by our unyielding confidence in the blood of Christ.

If we are having difficulty being confident that the blood of Christ has given us free access to the banquet of heaven, then desperate prayer may seem like the next best option – but that is not the way of the Spirit, that is the way of Adam.

The spirit has such an assurance of the efficacy of the blood of Christ that it *expects* it to do its work. It has not the slightest doubt, that by placing faith in it, it will achieve its goal. Prayer is the expression of the spirit's confidence – like asking Jesus to pass an item of food laid out at the banquet of heaven.

> **Prayer is simply a request which is saturated in confidence.**

Jesus has already made it clear that we are worthy guests at heaven's banquet. It is our rightful place because of our status as sons of God. Prayer is nothing more, and nothing less, than our participation in the outcomes of the cross – the bounty of heaven given back to us when Jesus declared 'it is finished'.

Adam (and his descendants) have spent such a long time looking for God, that now that we have found Him (or rather been found by Him), we don't know what to do with Him. So we have turned prayer into a continuum of Adams way – seeking the presence, power and favour of the one who has already hidden all of these things within us.

In Luke 18:1-8 the parable of the persistent widow is presented to us as the example for prayer. Jesus even recommended it as the model that we should always pray and not give up. The legacy of Adam is fully engaged at this point because it loves to play its part, yet, in verse 8 Jesus asks, "However, when the Son of Man comes, will He find faith on the earth?"

It seems to me that Jesus is not concerned about whether we will muster up persistence in prayer, but whether there will actually be any faith in it.

Jesus was speaking to people who were still under the Old Covenant law; they did not yet have His death on the cross to put their faith in. The only option open to them was the way of Adam *(get the staying power of human effort involved)*... but how sad is the lament that follows; will they manage to transition from persistence to faith – even after my resurrection, when they have my Spirit?

If they could only see the remarkable potential of my indwelling Spirit living in them, they would stop seeking me like their grandfather Adam, and rest in the certainty of my indwelling love.

Jesus looks ahead to the New Covenant in Matthew 6:7&8, "And when you pray, do not keep on babbling like pagans, for they think they will be heard because of their many words. Do not be like them, for your Father knows what you need before you ask Him". Then in 28–30 "And why do you worry about clothes? See how the flowers of the field grow. They do not labour or spin. Yet I tell you that not even Solomon in all his splendour was dressed like one of these. If that is how God clothes the grass of the field, which is here today and tomorrow is thrown into the fire, will He not much more clothe you—you of little faith?" My Father knows what you need before you ask Him. *Prayer and doubt do not mix!*

> **Faith is a New Covenant concept;**
> **it doesn't belong in the Old Covenant with Adam.**
> **The Old Covenant was fuelled by man's religious and lifestyle choices;**
> **the New Covenant is fuelled by faith in the blood of Christ.**

It's not that I'm against persistent prayer, it's that generally it doesn't spring from faith *(persistence seems at best, to be full of hope, as if the outcome is more connected to our determination than the certainty of the cross of Jesus)* – and Paul made it very clear in Romans 14:23, "That which is not of faith, is sin".

This is not about dampening our zeal for God, or disregarding Paul's encouragement to 'pray without ceasing', rather, it is about the fact that unless we learn to rest in the presence of the indwelling Christ, it is not physically possible to pray without ceasing. Only a revelation of the immediacy of the Spirit of God can produce a continuance of prayer – else we lapse into Adam's way, and attempt to raise up the flesh to an impossible task.

The sublime truth of the matter is that my spirit communes with God continually (without ceasing), and my soul leans back into this beautiful communion as it places confidence in the blood of Christ to carry it there.

CHAPTER 34

My Restful Design

I am continually in the same state as Adam was when he first opened his eyes and saw the love of God, my spirit cannot be distracted, such is His awesome glory.

This is the design of man… the perfect expression of the imagination of God.

But in spite of this, Adam had been pulled aside by the world – distracted, drawn away from his first love. He wanted to be someone special… *but he already was.*

Isn't it a strange paradox, that we can be so completely enveloped in the love and life of God, yet still feel the strong pull of the physical realm to define us? The flesh clamours for identity so strongly, that it is inclined to grasp hold of anything that gives it recognition and purpose.

The soul of man is not a divine mistake, God didn't accidently create us with this need for identity; it is very possibly the part of our being that best demonstrates God's creative flair. Yet this exceptional, wonderful part of us can only truly find fulfilment and identity when it rests in the divine union it has with God.

Satan took humanity down a road that he had already travelled himself; the compulsion to construct our identity from our independent being… *when we were designed by God to be united with Him.*

So if we are to embrace the sublime truth of our union again, and live in the wonder of it, we must resolve the pull of the physical realm. Otherwise, like Adam, we seek our 'specialness' in the wrong place.

The thing that makes us special (gives us identity) is that we are God's, and this is the thing that satan most wants to unsettle.

Perhaps the most troubling claim of the flesh is that God wants it to independently operate, *so that it can please God* by modelling back to Him the qualities that He values in Himself. Subtly, this is nothing short of setting ourselves up in God's place – the one who gives life and righteousness.

Identifying this subtle twist helps us to step back into our true identity.

Only God gives life. He alone is the source of all righteousness, and we are only complete when we cease from our striving and lose ourselves in Him. His identity then becomes ours, and our pursuit of self-generated worth is seen for what it really is – mere human effort masquerading as godliness.

That's why Paul uses such vivid language in Colossians 2:14, "having cancelled the charge of our legal indebtedness, which stood against us and condemned us; He has taken it away, nailing it to the cross". Paul wants to be sure we don't resurrect our Old Nature by giving it back the 'debt repayment role', which Adam first assigned to it.

Paul saw something that few see – that we don't please God by copying Jesus; we please God by hiding ourselves in Jesus. As we begin to rest in the sufficiency of the love of God expressed through Jesus, the life of Jesus takes us over – it really is the most sublime way to live, because every issue of our lives is carried by Him. We don't need to ask Him to, or present Him with a religiously impressive life – all we do is lean back into His goodness.

When we rest God works / when we work God rests.

At first it is surprising that 'resting' can achieve so much, but as we settle into this new way of living, a new kind of productivity comes forth. It's an unforced productivity which is the overflow of our faith in Jesus. Faith in Jesus shifts the spiritual work from us to Him, yet we are the ones who receive the benefit.

Sure, we keep busy – we continue to do all the things that responsible Christians do, but Jesus carries the load. He is the spiritual energy that powers us, so the outcome is His responsibility.

Each day is filled with activities that are unique to the design of our soul, our special way of expressing the fullness of God in us. We are completely satisfied and fulfilled as we live abundantly within the freedom of our unique design, yet the lightness of living abundantly is neither tiring nor burdensome, the load is so easy that there seems to be no burden at all.

Energetic living, without burden, equals rest.

In Colossians 1:29, "To this end I strenuously contend with all the energy Christ so powerfully works in me". Paul shows us how it's done. He doesn't slack off just because God is the powerhouse of his life; it actually propels him into a life of great service.

The energy that Christ so powerfully works in him is spiritual energy – it's the same energy that is behind the 'life' that Christ came to give us in John 10:10 *(ESV),* "I came that they may have life, and have it abundantly".

Paul worked with all the physical energy he could muster; he drove himself on because he had seen the magnificence of his salvation – and God provided the spiritual energy. Paul pushed himself in the natural realm, but he never carried the ultimate load because the end result was always dependant on the Holy Spirit.

It is one of the casualties of Adam's departure from the presence of God – Adam stepped out of this spiritual energy. He had to carry the load himself now, the abundant life of God was lost to him, it could only be found in the environment of the presence of God.

Adam knew he needed more than physical energy; something was missing that converted the physical energy into its intended result. It used to happen spontaneously when he dwelt in God's presence, that's the way God designed things – man provided the physical effort and God provided the spiritual life, and together they produced the desired outcome.

Remember in Genesis 2:15, "The Lord God took the man and put him in the Garden of Eden to work it and take care of it". Adam worked in the garden and the Lord caused the garden to grow. Adam rested in the life that God had placed in each seed and plant, he knew his only part was to work the garden and God would cause the life to come forth.

But once he had left the presence of God something changed, Genesis 3:17-19 *(BSB)* "Cursed is the ground because of you; in toil you will eat of it all the days of your life. Both thorns and thistles it shall grow for you;

and you will eat the plants of the field; by the sweat of your face you will eat bread, till you return to the ground".

God did not change the nature of the earth; it remained just as God had made it, but the curse of 'human effort' now hung over it – restful labour had turned into toil and sweat.

Without the ability to lean-in to the Spirit of God as the source of his life, Adam had to self-generate an alternative. He began to look to his soul to provide the life that had previously flowed freely from the Spirit of God.

His emotions attempted to step into the role of the Spirit, and so began the fretful existence that has defined humanity ever since – 'Will everything be alright?', 'Will I have enough money?', 'Will my effort produce the result I am hoping for?'

It was exhausting, it was emotionally draining, and it was the exact opposite of our original design.

"And why do you worry about clothes? See how the flowers of the field grow. They do not labour or spin. Yet I tell you that not even Solomon in all his splendour was dressed like one of these. If that is how God clothes the grass of the field, which is here today and tomorrow is thrown into the fire, will He not much more clothe you—you of little faith?"

CHAPTER 35

Courage

Jesus has returned us to our original design. The 'abundant life' that Jesus came to give us is ours again if we chose to live by the unforced ways of the Spirit.

But it takes courage.

> *God can't give us courage; it is not His to give –*
> *we must choose to abandon ourselves to something we cannot see.*
> *Only we can do it. Only we can have courage.*

All of the spiritual talk, Christian clichés and pious rhetoric do not equate to it. The courage that is required does not spring from the cultural things we have gathered up from this great big thing called Christianity – it can only be gained by a thorough examination of the cross of Christ. We must keep considering it and asking God what it was all about, so that, ultimately, we become so convinced of its truth that we let go of our self-made props, and courageously cling to Jesus for everything.

This courage ushers in a new life.

We are actually exercising courage against the pull of the flesh; we are denying the loud insistence of Adam's legacy and putting our trust in a less audible, but far superior voice.

John 6:63 says, "The Spirit gives life; the flesh counts for nothing" – but the flesh doesn't take it lying down. It takes all our courage to turn away from the demands of the flesh and fix our faith on the cross of Jesus.

Faith and courage are close relatives; they are part of the same family, lifelong companions.

I have heard some people say they have faith, but if they don't have the courage to entrust their entire existence into the object of their faith, then it's not really faith at all – just a hopeful longing.

The kind of faith which is accompanied by courage is uncommon in my observation. The modern Christian culture has produced its own version of faith. It has the outward appearance of faith, but is more anchored in Adam's way than the Spirits way. It is optimistic, demonstrative and upbeat – *but it isn't certain.*

This counterfeit of true faith takes the best of human effort, and inserts it in the place of the best of Christ. But human qualities do not move God, only the blood of Christ can impress him. Real faith, the kind that can move the mountains in our lives, has conducted a thorough examination of the cross of Christ. It has determined once and for all that the certainty of the cross can be trusted, and has then transferred all of its confidence across. It takes real courage to exercise that kind of faith.

It need not be overly demonstrative, because it springs from rest not from human effort. It is based on an assurance *that Jesus has completed something already*, rather than *that God will do something in response to us.*

The beauty of this courage/faith is that anyone can have it.

We don't need to be physically strong or intellectual. Nor do we need to be a spiritual leader or have a ministry. All we need to do is consider the cross of Christ, and determine that it was enough. In fact, the weak and lowly are often more likely to exercise this true faith, because they have already accepted that their inner resources are limited.

The biblical statement, 'The first shall be last, and the last shall be first' is proven to be true when those whom the world considers to be losers, rise up and exercise this faith in spite of their circumstances.

Those who live in this place of courage/faith may be very old, or very young, frail even and poor, but they are the explorers of a new frontier. They ride the boundaries of the heart of God, opening up new territory for the settlers that follow.

Much of Adam's version of Christianity is preoccupied with circling around this courage/faith instead of exploring its horizons. It prefers to continue asking God to give and do things which have already been released to us at the cross. It prefers to put the onus back onto God's initiative, instead of our own faith.

Remember Peter and John's response to the lame beggar in Acts 3:6 "Silver or gold I do not have, but what I do have I give you. In the name of Jesus Christ of Nazareth, walk." They knew what they had, and they gave it to the beggar – they didn't go to God for a miracle, but courageously assumed the initiative and gave the lame beggar his healing themselves.

The blood of Christ calls out to us, 'Be of great courage, do not fear, for I will never leave you nor forsake you'. And a few hear the call, their spiritual ears prick-up at the sound of His voice. Faint at first, then becoming clear. It is a voice that calls us, and woos, drawing us out of our self-imposed captivity to doubt, and into the adventure of the Spirit – the adventure we were made for.

The adventure is not what you think; it's not about going to exotic places and mixing with the diverse and strange people of faraway lands, it's much closer to home. This is an adventure of the heart. Sure, there may be other adventures which overflow from this one into the far flung corners of the world, but this is the real adventure. This is where it all begins.

The voice that has captured our hearing calls us to do the impossible, believe the impossible. It calls us to let go of doubt – *the most human of all traits,* because, after doubt has been subdued by faith, the whole world opens up to us.

> ***Doubt didn't exist at first,***
> ***Adam created it when he embarked on his mad experiment –***
> ***it was a direct result of depending upon himself,***
> ***which is the most doubtful of all enterprises.***

This adventure of the heart is daring. It pioneers a way of living which defies all our natural instincts; it stakes its claim into the richest of all goldfields – the holiness and love of God. Against all the odds and all the doubters, this pioneering soul lays its claim to the most perfect nature of all heaven. It grasps the impossible, and steps into a perfection that it did not earn or contribute to whatsoever – it assumes the right to be a son of God.

'Sonship' implies a level of esteem which grates upon the legacy of Adam. Sonship is by birthright, not by self-imposed servitude – it is 'inborn' rather than earned. This adventurous son of God takes the term 'born-again' to a whole new level; he assumes that the term means he is literally heavenly royalty, with all of the rights and privileges that it implies.

He steps around all of the obligations that Adam invented as the human contribution to this status, and courageously assumes upon the word of God and the blood of Christ. This is the true courage of the heart.

This courageous one has made an inner determination; I am not the sum total of my human attributes, my intelligence, creativity, beauty or wealth *(or the lack of them)*. I am a son of the Living God, made so by the blood of Christ. This is the new and real me. No one can take this identity from me. The realm of nature did not give it to me, and it cannot take it away. I am of a higher order, I am of God.

The adventure of the heart is one of assuming our new identity. It takes great courage to assume such a status in opposition to the doubtful murmurings of the crowd. The crowd know who we have been – they know our past, our failings and foibles, and they look at the natural evidence instead of the capacity of the blood of Christ to perform the impossible.

…the adventurous one goes ahead anyway.

There is a boldness that borders on recklessness, a presumption upon the blood of Christ shed 2000 years ago to transform the nature of Adam's descendant in the here and now – this really is the stuff of a much higher order.

While those of the lower order are fighting to keep afloat, struggling and even dying in their attempts to hold on to a semblance of well-being, the inhabitants of the higher order are at rest in the life of Christ. Not that they cease to be mindful of the earthly struggles that are raging all around them, but that their hearts have moved on to safer ground – and so they relate to the world as visitors, not permanent residents.

CHAPTER 36
Eternity

Everything we now do has eternity stamped on it. Time cannot hold us, or our actions, into the limitations of our present tense lives. All that we are and do is eternal – any expression of the life of Christ within us contains His supernatural eternal life. What I mean is that the same 'life' that Jesus came to give us in John 10:10, is now the divine energy behind all we do.

What a beautiful thing, to think that our words and actions are eternal.

Adam bookended our actions between birth and death, but Jesus released us from Adam's limitations and gave us back eternity, *even while we are seeing out our remaining years on earth.* The life of Christ in us is like that, it is eternally consequential. Always loving, always bringing life. It is Jesus doing over and over again what He has always done – giving life to men through His indwelling presence in humankind.

He is LIFE, and He is in us.

John 5:24 speaks of this new reality, "Very truly I tell you, whoever hears my word and believes Him who sent me has eternal life and will not be judged but *has crossed over* from death to life". We do not arrive at this new reality at the end of our physical lives, but rather, in the moment when we believe we are released from the limitation of time, and translated into eternity.

And now that we have eternal life everything we do has the divine vitality of eternity stamped on it.

But I must add a caveat; not every Christian lives out their lives from this new reality. It has been fully transacted and deposited into every believer, *but we must choose to live there.* Every believer is exactly the same regarding their status as eternal beings. As Colossians 1:13 puts it, "We have been brought into the kingdom of the Son He loves", but we only live from the resources of eternity when we put our faith in the fact that it is now our home.

When we make a study of this new reality, we find that it is referenced all through the New Testament. Our condition as 'strangers and aliens', 'our new nature in Christ', and 'Christ in us', our heavenly position 'seated with God', these are all woven through the pages. Yet, the eyes of Adam missed these glorious truths, because these truths minimise the resources of humanity and draw upon the resources of eternity.

The soul of man is finally back where it belongs, drawing life from the indwelling presence of one much higher than itself. It can only discover its true self when it draws upon the vitality of Christ as the source of its being, rather than its own efforts to self-generate goodness.

And when it does,
when it finally stops fighting the reality of Christ within,
a beautiful thing happens –
the supernatural life of Christ overflows out of that person,
into a world that is hungry for reality.

Religion has attempted to counterfeit this spontaneous overflow of the life of Christ. Such statements as 'We are God's hands and feet' have a ring of truth to them, but when these actions spring from a sense of obligatory servitude, they are nothing more than the deeds of Adam masquerading as spirituality. We are sons, not servants. The kingdom belongs to us and we distribute its assets by resting in our inborn status – a servant does not own the estate and does not have the right to give away its assets, all a servant can do is follow orders. A son, however, operates from a completely different position, he gives what he owns. He gives the realities of eternity to a needy world.

Once again the example of Peter and John comes to mind, "Silver or gold I do not have, but what I do have I give you. In the name of Jesus Christ of Nazareth, walk." They knew what they had as sons in God's estate – they didn't go to God for a miracle, but simply gave what they owned. They gave the lame beggar his healing because Jesus had given it them to distribute as they saw fit.

A servant can only give away the resources of Adam, it is all they have. Like Adam, the best they can offer is self-generated acts of goodness, expressed as physical actions into Adams time-based world. Adam re-made humanity to operate from its own resources, this is programmed into all humanity, it is all that humanity knew.

A son has all of the resources of eternity at his disposal. The supernatural presence of God is his daily fare. He lives by faith in the life giving flow which proceeds from the heart of God – this flow does not require Adam's self-effort, it is activated by faith in the life of Christ.

Jesus explained the difference to the woman at the well in John 4:13-14, Jesus said to her, "Everyone who drinks this water will be thirsty again. But whoever drinks the water I give him will never thirst. Indeed, the water I give him will become in him a fount of water springing up to eternal life."

The water that Adam gives can only give a momentary time-based benefit. It quenches our thirst in the here and now. But the water Jesus gives has eternity in it – we are never thirsty again when we drink of it (He is the river of life). We also give this same eternal water to the thirsty souls of humanity when we believe in the life of Christ within – it is a bubbling spring of life that is delivered from the heart of God into a thirsty world.

The redeemed human soul is a now conduit or channel – life flows from the vitality of the spiritual realm (our spirit in perfect union with God's Spirit), out into the natural realm through us. The soul no longer needs to try and produce its own life, now it is simply a fountain head which pours forth the life of God.

When the soul rests in this divine flow, everything it does has eternal life within it.

Every thought and deed, every prayer and desire, is like the light of God, leaking out of us into the world. We do not have to do anything to activate this flow of light, but keep our eyes fixed on the light. Hebrews 12:2 *(NAS)* tells us, "Fixing our eyes on Jesus, the author and perfector of our faith". He will write upon our lives the most magnificent story of His light shining through us as we allow Him to be the author. He perfects our faith as we fix our eyes on His love expressed at the cross.

Yes, even our prayer life has eternity within it as we lean back into the love of God. In the past we may have brought our petitions to God, reaching out to Him for help, asking and even begging Him for His touch upon the lives of His people – reaching up from the helplessness of the natural realm to the resources of the spiritual realm.

But as eternity seeps into our prayer life, faith springs up. We begin to distribute the bountiful feast of God's banquet from our new eternal home out into the natural realm. We don't ask God for permission, that was given to us a long time ago at the cross. We simply cast our eyes around the lavish love of God which is our new environment, and give it to a needy world.

Our prayer is not conditional upon God's will or His eternal plan for mankind – that was already fully expressed at the cross. He is willing; His plan is that we would feast at His banquet. He invites us to come and be filled by the bread of life – *Jesus himself*. Jesus removed the conditions at the cross; we are now invited guests to the extravagance of God.

In Mark 11:24 Jesus puts it out there, "Therefore I tell you, whatever you ask for in prayer, believe that you have received it, and it will be yours". *No conditions; just belief.*

This kind of belief was too big a hurdle for Adam to jump. He couldn't see how he could leap over his human frailties into such confidence – doubt always held him back.

Jesus has leaped over the bar for us. Now we can believe, just like Adam did in the very beginning. Now we can open our eyes and be filled with the radiance of God's love. A love that lifts us above doubt, all the way into eternity where there is no doubting. And our faith is perfected as we fix our gaze on the lavish love of God, expressed through Jesus.

This doubt free existence is the purpose of our salvation.

But we cannot have it by sheer determination. It is a not a thing of positive thinking, nor is it something we muster up from our hope-based inner reserves. It is impossible for the faith that moves mountains to be produced by the earth based initiatives of man.

James made this very clear in chapter 1:6-8, "But when you ask, you must believe and not doubt, because the one who doubts is like a wave of the sea, blown and tossed by the wind. That person should not expect to receive anything from the Lord. Such a person is double-minded and unstable in all they do". It doesn't matter who we are, it is simply not possible to generate this kind of faith from our own resources – we don't have it within us.

Religion has taught us to measure the substance of our faith according to the well-being we experience in our circumstances, but the Spirit looks beyond the issues of life to the well-being of our spirit in its union with Jesus. Our circumstances are not our greatest reality, and we must not allow them to compete with our true existence in Christ as the foundation of our confidence.

The only way is to look away from ourselves and our circumstance, and away from the earthly counterfeit of sheer determination and zeal, and fix our eyes on Christ. When we take-in the vista of the cross of Christ, anything is possible. We find our hearts translated out of the natural realm, and into the supernatural realm, where the power of God is available on tap.

'Faith that does not doubt' is not characteristic of broken humanity – it is not in us since Adam's mutiny. We can only gain such faith by feeding on the Tree of Life (Jesus) again.

CHAPTER 37

The Cross

'Faith that does not doubt' is not found in the self-focussed religious system that fallen humanity developed. God is not looking over the banisters of heaven hoping that someone will stir up enough spiritual guts and determination to get the job done. Quite the opposite, He wants us to stop trying so hard and rest in the spiritual work already accomplished by Jesus.

> *God wants us to believe in Jesus*
> *– not in our own earthly determination.*

What I mean by this is that our gaze should always be upon the sufficiency of the cross, not on our own attempts to get God's attention. We do not change the earthly problem by giving it our intensity and self-generated determination. Instead, we apply the work of the cross to it by treating it as it really is – an earthly matter that wants to elevate itself above the blood of Christ and rob us of our inheritance.

We do not give undue attention to satan, he is already defeated. If we fix our gaze upon satan and attempt to subdue him by our self-made spiritual guts and determination, then all we are doing is re-fighting a battle that Christ already won.

> *We rest in Christ's victory; we do not fight it for Him.*

This is not a passive thing; it is actually the strongest power we can exercise. By resting we are making use of the same power which raised Jesus from the dead.

In fact, it is not a thing that is especially concerned with 'what we do' – it is more closely related to 'where we live'.

If we can see that Christ has reset us to our original design, and relocated us back to our original habitation, then the eternal life of God will flow out of us. It will be uncontainable because the Holy Spirit will no longer be restricted by the man that Adam made, and the life of God no longer be held back by the frailties of humanity.

Never before had I contemplated the prospect that the sacrifice of Christ had produced such a dramatic outcome. I had always contained Him into my environment, instead of losing myself in His environment. So, my salvation (though real and personal to a degree), was only ever a fraction of its true scale. I had limited God into my man-sized thinking.

I had inadvertently jumped on-board with Adam's way of doing life. Even though I had received the salvation offered to me by Jesus, I had neatly contained it within the thinking of Adam – *the thinking that made that salvation necessary in the first place.*

And the words of Jesus in Luke 18:8 echoed through my mind, "However, when the son of man comes, will He find faith on the earth?" It seems to me that we are actually perpetuating the very thing that Jesus prophesied. He looked ahead and knew the way humanity would respond to His gospel – *we would gratefully receive it, and then re-hide it in the thinking of Adam.*

If this book is about anything, it is about uncovering the gospel of Jesus all over again. It is about dragging it out of the thinking of Adam, and re-establishing it squarely in the mind of Christ where it belongs.

The big question we started with, "Is my faith really representative of the way God meant it to be?" continues to loom before us, but now we have some material to actually deal with that question.

So it begs the next question, "Will we do something with the first question?"

It's easy for me to ask the questions, but not so easy to get them answered.

Jesus asked questions too – "When the son of man returns will He find faith on the earth?"

The 80/20 rule seems to apply – 20% of the people control the answers for the other 80%. But, the answers matter to the 80%, because there's a chance the 20% could be wrong. Jesus must have thought the 20% could be wrong too, or else His question would never have been necessary.

And I wonder if that question also now falls into the category of 'The things that will not return to Him void'. It's an eternal question, 'Will the son of man find faith on the earth?' It resonates through time and eternity, calling us to risk everything and agree with God.

The things of which I am speaking are foreign to us – foreign to our natural way, foreign to our natural mind. They call us out of the land we know, the land we have grown-up in, and into a land of mystery.

The mind of God is different to the one we thought He had. He calls us out of the mindset we have grown up in, and into His own mysterious and foreign mind. It is a mind where a 'thought' is the same as a 'fact', and a prayer is answered before it is uttered. It is so foreign that we can't imagine living there – yet we were made for it.

We were made for the same eternal consciousness as God.

CHAPTER 38
My Name

But first my new name; the one that belonged to my spirit before Adam cut us all loose to a world were names are given on account of our place in humanity. Our new name is the one God calls us by; it is an eternal name that describes our uniquely perfect soul, clothed in the divinity of God.

God seems to have a habit of giving people names, and changing their earthly name to a new eternal one. He sees the potential of the life of Jesus within us, and names us accordingly.

You shall be called…….

It fits me, it is me – I am named by God.

A name that combines His divinity, with the unique genius of the soul that He made for me. A special name for me alone, but one that is known throughout all of heaven, because heaven is my home and all that live there know that He loves me.

> *And when He says my name I am complete –*
> *love has been spoken, and it will not return to Him void.*

God speaks a word, and I am, and He is pleased with me – He sees that I am good, just as He planned before I was formed in my mother's womb.

Isaiah 55:11 *(NKJV),* "So shall my word be that goes forth out of my mouth: it shall not return to me void, but it shall accomplish that which I please, and it shall prosper in the thing I sent it to do". The word of God has accomplished me; it did what it was sent to do.

But more than that, this word (my name from God), resonates through eternity forever and ever. I am held by it, empowered by it, and made holy by it.

Jesus is the Living Word, 'In the beginning was the *Word*' and He sustains all things by His powerful word. Hebrews 1:3, "The Son is the radiance of God's glory and the exact representation of His being, sustaining all things by His powerful *word*. After He had provided purification for sins, He sat down at the right hand of the Majesty in heaven".

Jesus sustains me in the righteousness of God. He sits down at the right hand of God's majesty and my name is heard throughout heaven for all eternity... *'This one is the object of God's love, he is precious to the Father, he is fearfully and wonderfully made – a perfect creation of the heart of God'.*

"Will the son of man find faith on the earth?" Yes, He most certainly will!

Faith rises in me as I hear my name resonating through heaven. I am meant to be here, this is not just a cosmic coincidence. I am of the Father's heart – I can see it now... *and faith wells-up in me.*

The 20% are wrong. They said I was the sum of my best deeds, they said my name was earthly. But now I see what they missed – I am the overflow of the heart of God. He spoke my name in the beginning, before I was even formed in my mother's womb, and His words do not return to Him empty. I am His because He spoke His divine nature in to me in the beginning, and the Living Word spoke it back into me at the cross.

Jesus returned God's word to Him... God has got me again.

It comes as a surprise that the further my heart journeys into my true identity in God, the less I feel like a foreigner here. And, better still, the more I feel as though I am floating a little above the circumstances of life on earth.

Whatever fills my screen – is where I am.

As I begin to hear God saying my name, I am more and more captivated by His presence. A new balance seems to be slowly overtaking me. My spirit is taking over, and my soul is leaning in too. I am learning to walk as God first made me to, when He spoke my name into eternity. The harmony between my spirit and my soul is restored again, as they are released to be true to the eternal name God gave me.

My new name is as much about God as it is about me. It is like looking in a mirror and seeing God reflected back to me. I have no identity apart from God; our union is so seamless, so blended, that there is no me, without God.

My soul relishes this new way. It fits, and it is as light as a feather. My soul revels in the fact that it is no longer required to generate righteousness. Instead, it receives righteousness by resting in the word God has spoken. The scripture Psalm 55:22 comes to mind, "Cast your cares on the Lord and He will sustain you; He will never let the righteous be shaken", and another like it Matthew 11:29-30, "Take my yoke upon you and learn from me; for I am gentle and humble in heart, and you will find rest for your souls. For my yoke is easy and my burden is light."

My soul has found its rest.

The question I have been asking in this book is all about the soul. The spirit is doing just fine – it has been relocated into the presence of God, it couldn't be happier... *and my soul is catching on too!*

CHAPTER 39
Two Voices

My soul hears two voices – the Spirit of Jesus and way of Adam. The Spirit speaks out of the spiritual realm, and Adam speaks out of the natural realm. The Spirit speaks words of life, Adam speaks words of death.

We instinctively know this, it is not actually new information, it's just been buried so deep inside us that we have lost the ability to process it. The ability to lay hold of the words of life that the Spirit speaks to us has been hidden by the ruckus of Adam, the incessant noise of the natural realm all but drowns out the most liberating message ever spoken to humanity.

And when we do hear it, it is quickly swallowed up by the rationale of the earthly broadcast.

The reason it can be so easily swallowed up by Adam's way, is that the Spirit's way seems too good to be true. Adam re made the soul of humanity to doubt good news, we are more inclined towards bad tidings, they seem to rest more easily in the frailties of humanity.

But when God first spoke our names into eternity, our destiny was set, and the decision by Adam to remake humanity became irrelevant. God had spoken, and the matter was closed. It is unthinkable to consider that a word spoken from the heart of God would return empty – that Adam had more power to give us a name, than God.

We may well think that satan is closer to the truth in assigning an earthly name to us, and that the evidence is very much in his favour, but we must understand that evidence in the natural realm is inferior to a word from the heart of God.

If God has given us a name, then that is our name. Satan can call us what he likes, he may even convince us (and the crowd that knows us), that his name is the right name for us, but satan's deception does not cancel out God's word, we are who God says we are.

Our destiny is in God's hands, not satan's.

Remember the verse in Hebrews, "Never will I leave you, never will I forsake you". We have been listening to the wrong voice the whole time. God has spoken, and our destiny is held firm by His word. Our eternal name, the name that He wrote in His book, cannot be changed just because Adam had other ideas. Christ came to rewrite human history – He will never leave me nor forsake me.

Think of all the references to Jesus that use the word 'Life'. 'I am the Way, the Truth, and the Life', 'In Him was Life and that Life was the light of men', 'I came that you might have Life'. **Jesus is Life.** It radiates from every pore of His being, and He has kept a record of those who received His life – He wrote their names on His own heart. He is the Book of Life, and our eternal names are written in His blood.

> *Jesus wrote my name back into the eternal record,*
> *the name that the Father gave me in the beginning,*
> *and now it lives on for all eternity in my unbreakable union with Jesus.*

My parentage has been resolved. I had felt myself being pulled in two directions, but now I know that I am of the King's family. I am born of the royal blood line, my lineage is ancient and eternal – I just didn't realise it until now.

The question was never one of earning my place. I was born into royalty; I am of the King's line. The question was always about whether I would assume the magnitude of my lineage.

'Is my faith really representative of the way God meant it to be?'… I can no longer settle for the scaled down version of myself that Adam came up with. It would be an offence to the high price that Jesus paid for me, when he purchased me back for God. My destiny was in God's hands, and He has handed it back to me – and now no one can keep me from my inheritance but myself.

Now that I know who I am, I must now also learn how to live in this foreign land of God's goodness.

My soul is not a despicable thing to God. It does not *in itself* give any offence; it is only as it assumes the role of 'life-giving' that it takes on a persona which is out of place in God's presence. My soul is the unique 'me' that God created, and the thing I must learn is how to simply be 'me', without having to depend on myself as the 'life-source' of my being.

My soul has been set free from the obligation to generate life, but what does it do now that it is free?

It is helpful to reflect on my royal status. I did not create this status, nor did I earn it – but, now that I know I have it, how do I live?

CHAPTER 40

Unburdened

All my soul has ever known is the burden of self-generated righteousness, a burden heavier than any other load ever placed on the bent-over shoulders of humanity, because it robs us of ourselves.

This new burden of Jesus is so light that my back can straighten again. Now I can look up, I can see the wonders of life before me, the vista of 'no condemnation' is more expansive than I had ever imagined, and my soul is set free into it.

Now that condemnation has been lifted off, my soul can enter into the life it was made for. I am a son of the King (a prince of heaven), and the wonders of God's goodness, a land that had been foreign to me for so long, is mine to discover.

Religion promotes sameness. It moulds people into conformity, and denies us our uniqueness. Living in the freedom of our unique design can seem too extravagant and self-indulgent at first, but that's because the echo of Adam's fears still reaches our ears. The whole point of 'no-condemnation' is that we live large, and that the fear of 'getting it wrong' disappears in our wake as we set sail with the Holy Spirit as our navigator.

Many are reluctant to embark on this journey for fear that they might not hear the Holy Spirit's voice, or that they might mistake it for their own ambitions, or, worse still, the deception of satan. But the adventure of the heart requires us to cast caution to the wind, and trust that the Holy Spirit will get through to us because He knows how to communicate with every unique soul that was created from the heart of God.

John 10:27 *(ESV)* says, "My sheep hear my voice, and I know them, and they follow me". The Holy Spirit will lead us, and we will hear His voice, even if we feel that our lives so far have been spent in spiritual deafness.

The reason many feel that they don't hear from the Holy Spirit is because they are expecting Him to tell them what to do. But the Holy Spirit is not so concerned with that, He wants to tell us who we are, and then, when we get it, the doing will take care of itself.

Many well-intended Christians wait patiently for the Holy Spirits instructions, as though the Holy Spirit is the one that determines the course their life should take. But that is not how the divine navigator works. Instead, He shows us the magnificence of our salvation, the wonders of God's love, and the flow of holiness between God's heart and ours, and then He waits for the penny to drop. We are free to discover Life. We have been released to live our own version of God's abundance. It is not limited by the Holy Spirit's directions, but our view of what we are in.

And He gently touches our life so that our gaze remains fixed on Jesus.

The Holy Spirit does not cast us loose to randomly drift through life, it's not like that. He reveals to us the potential of our union with Jesus to accomplish much more than we ever hoped or dreamed possible. If we can see that, then no action, no word, no prayer will ever return to us void.

This is the soul of humankind at its best. Living above the pull of condemnation, upon the wings of God's goodness, expecting the sacrifice of Jesus to accomplish much in our lives, and to transform those people and circumstances we touch.

It is a daring life because it has grasped the truth of God's love and cast itself completely into its fidelity, expecting, without thought for any alternative, that it will achieve the outcome it was sent for.

There is no doubt now, because the outcome is not dependant on my self-generated goodness or religious effort. It rests entirely on Jesus, and it is bold because it has come face-to-face with His love, and is convinced it can be counted on. If there was the smallest element of my virtue involved then doubt would be my undoing, but it is all Jesus – I am simply the vehicle of His love.

Doubts that spring from thoughts of unworthiness, or from God's remoteness, are out of place in this new land. Being confident in the fact that 'God has got me' is the air that I breathe; it is the source of all that I do.

The navigator is doing what He does, John 15:26 *(NHE)*, "But when the Helper comes, whom I will send to you from the Father, the Spirit of truth, who proceeds from the Father, He will testify about me".

> **Jesus called himself 'The Way',
> and the Holy Spirit's job is to navigate us to Jesus.**

If we can see that we are hidden in the work of Christ then the navigator has done His job, because then the life of Christ will carry us into our destiny.

The way of Adam is at last seen for the madness that it is, and the way of Jesus is my new sanity. The old way is now becoming a foreigner to me as I tentatively step out into my new nature. It is like a breath of fresh air after being cooped up in the closet of my fears. Boldness is nearer, and confidence is coming to me more easily as my eyes are learning not to waver from the light – *the light that holds my destiny.*

Scriptures I have known all my life are at last starting to make sense, like 1 John 1:7, "But if we walk in the light, as He is in the light, we have fellowship with one another, and the blood of Jesus, His Son, purifies us from all sin" – my only part is to walk in the light, Christ does everything else.

This 'walking' has a way of shutting out time, past failures are forgotten, and so are future fears. There is only the present, and the presence of light. My destiny is assured because past and future are no longer my master; I have been hidden in the ever present reality of eternity.

Everything is hidden in Christ. Colossians 1:15-17 says, "The Son is the image of the invisible God, the firstborn over all creation. For in Him all things were created, things in heaven and on earth, visible and invisible, whether thrones or dominions or rulers or authorities. All things were created through Him and for Him. He is before all things, and in Him all things hold together...."

There is nothing beyond the reach of His redemptive work on the cross. Nothing past, nothing future – all things have been created by Him, and for Him, and in Him they hold together. As I walk in the light, the truth about Jesus becomes clear, He purifies everything by His word, and He purifies me. He does it... *and I simply walk Him around.*

He shines out of me… that is the design and destiny of my soul.

In that way, my spirit and my soul have become one. The union that my spirit enjoys with Jesus is expressed by Jesus through my soul, and the circle of God's love is complete.

My soul has found its destiny and the genius of God is expressed through me. It wasn't created for independence, but deep dependence – a deep union which leans-in to the love and goodness of God, and discovers to its great surprise that the new commandment is the spontaneous overflow. I can love as Christ first loved me, because now He expresses His love through me.

I agree with God at last.

Conclusion

I have deliberately referred to the soul and the spirit as separate entities just as the bible does. The man which Adam handed on to humankind was indeed divided into these two completely individual and unrelated parts.

The work that Jesus accomplished on the cross was the reunifying of ourselves, such that we can now have a seamless union between spirit and soul. This seamless reunion has been fully enacted by Christ, and the damage to humanity caused by Adam has been repaired.

Jesus has perfected the whole of me. My spirit and my soul are inseparable forever.

God's design was that the spirit, and the soul, and the body of a man would be in perfect harmony. It was not His intention for man to perceive himself as made up of separate parts, each vying for identity, but one beautifully balanced being, in perfect union with Himself.

When two dancers come together and waltz, they appear to be one entity – so perfectly do they lead and follow that they have become one – no longer two people dancing, but one display of perfection.

As the soul is liberated from the obligation to do everything (both lead and follow), the dance begins, and the soul leans-in to the spirit's blissful union with God. Life flows spontaneously from the wonder of knowing, and being known by God. This is what we were made for, the sheer perfection of being the object of God's love.

> ***God likes me; He is pleased with His work,***
> ***and I am now free to live as the delight of His heart.***

And He likes you too! He likes all of us so much that He spent the life of Jesus so that Adam's way could be crucified, and we could become our true selves again.

The question that remains is this: Do we think God is that good? Do we agree with Him?

And are we ready to abandon ourselves to His design once again? By allowing the revelation which comes from our spirit's union with God, to become our life-defining truth.

He has always known what He is doing; He has loved us for eternity... *dare we abandon ourselves to such extravagant love?*

Cheers, Graeme.

www.ingramcontent.com/pod-product-compliance
Lightning Source LLC
Chambersburg PA
CBHW070603010526
44118CB00012B/1440